The EU's Common Foreign and Security Policy

This book reorients the study of European foreign and security policy towards the question of democracy. Blending insights from international relations and democratic theory, it aims to enhance our understanding of the issues at stake. The main structures, the institutional setting and the procedures that govern decision-making in this domain are examined. In this way, the book supplements studies with a more traditional focus on the substance of foreign policy. What are the democratic challenges in this distinct field of policy-making?

The Common Foreign and Security Policy (CFSP) of the European Union (EU) is usually assumed to be intergovernmental. Contributors to this book examine the extent to which a move beyond intergovernmentalism has taken place, how this manifests itself, and what may be the democratic implications. While the EU's international outlook testifies to a quest for democracy, the institutions and procedures that govern decision-making are found wanting.

This book was originally published as a special issue of *Journal of European Public Policy*.

Helene Sjursen is Professor at ARENA – Centre for European Studies, University of Oslo, Norway; she has been at ARENA since 1997. Her main fields of academic interest include the EU as an international actor, EU's foreign and security policy and EU enlargement.

Journal of European Public Policy Series
Series Editor: Jeremy Richardson is a Professor at Nuffield College, Oxford University

This series seeks to bring together some of the finest edited works on European Public Policy. Reprinting from Special Issues of the *Journal of European Public Policy*, the focus is on using a wide range of social sciences approaches, both qualitative and quantitative, to gain a comprehensive and definitive understanding of Public Policy in Europe.

The EU's Common Foreign and Security Policy

The Quest for Democracy

Edited by
Helene Sjursen

Routledge
Taylor & Francis Group

LONDON AND NEW YORK

Contents

The EU's Common Foreign and Security Policy: the quest for democracy

Helene Sjursen

ABSTRACT   This collection seeks to reorient studies of European foreign and security policy towards the question of democracy. The aim is to blend insights from international relations and democratic theory in order to enhance our understanding of what is at stake.

Calls for more powers to the European Parliament (EP) in the European Union's (EU) foreign and security policy (CFSP/ESDP) are becoming increasingly common. How can this be? Even with the Lisbon Treaty, foreign and security policy is said to remain intergovernmental, with state territory as the core organizing principle for its institutions.[1] In such a context, sustaining national democratic procedures that enable the accountability of executives should not be a problem. Why, then, the allegation of a democratic deficit and the demand for increased powers to the EP?

In this collection we critically examine the claim of an emerging democratic deficit in the field of foreign and security policy. In order to do so, it is necessary to have a clearer picture of the degree and form of integration in this domain. It is only when this is clarified that we can establish what kinds of democratic problems – if any – may have arisen. If the EU has moved beyond intergovernmentalism, questions would arise as to how national executives can be held accountable. However, a departure from intergovernmentalism does not necessarily point in a single direction, and different forms of integration would require different forms and channels of democratic legitimation. Hence, this collection follows a twin track of addressing both the questions of the 'nature of the beast' and of democracy.

A number of important attempts have been made at conceptualizing EU foreign and security policy. A first generation of scholars, focusing on the coherence of policies, discussed the extent to which the EU might be referred to as a foreign policy 'actor', or whether it was rather a 'presence', or perhaps a 'flop' (Sjøstedt 1977; Hill 1990; Allen and Smith 1990). Further conceptualizations

1

range from 'civilian power' (Duchêne 1972; Smith 2000) to 'empire' (Zielonka 2006) and 'superpower' (Galtung 1973; McCormick 2007). These conceptual efforts share in a focus on substance. They mainly seek to draw conclusions regarding the polity from the nature of its policies. Hence, they argue, in line with realist-empiricist traditions, that in order to establish what the EU 'is' one must look at what it 'does'.

In this contribution the starting point is different. The main focus is on the main structures, the institutional setting and the procedures that govern decision-making processes in this domain. The aim is to identify any putative democratic challenges through analyses of the institutions and procedures that mark out foreign policy as a distinct field of policy-making. This is important, as questions of legitimacy are not only linked to policy content. From the perspective of democratic legitimacy, a key question is to what extent procedures that may ensure that the viewpoints of all those affected by decisions may be heard are in place. Ultimately, those that abide by the law should also be seen as its authors.

In recent years, authors have highlighted what has been termed a process of 'Brusselsization' of European foreign and security policy (Allen 1998). There has been a shift in the locus of national decision-making to Brussels-based institutional structures. This might mean that, in spite of formally safeguarding the sovereign right of member states to veto any decision with which they disagree, the member states have in practice entered a slippery slope of integration with decision-making competence 'creeping' to Brussels. If the Brussels-based institutions are seen to 'gain the advantage' owing to, for example, easy and daily access to information and dialogue with partner states, this might point towards a more autonomous foreign and security policy for the EU. Such developments may have implications for democracy – as there would be something at the EU level that requires legitimation. However, institutions and decision-making in the CFSP are rarely analysed from this perspective.[2]

More research is required in order to assess the implications of the ongoing transformation of institutions and decision-making procedures both for our understanding of the CFSP as intergovernmental and for core democratic principles. To be sure, there is a considerable body of literature on the role and powers of the European Parliament (Crum 2006; Thym 2006; Wagner 2006). However, this literature must be complemented by analyses of the institutional system seen as a whole. There is a need to ascertain the authority of those who make decisions, identify their location within the overall system of European foreign and security policy, and find out to whom they render account. Research might also aim to uncover possible processes, pathways, points of access or meeting places that may allow for input from citizens or their representatives, for public deliberation or accountability at the EU level in this domain. The call for such analyses does not prejudge the question of efficiency, or presume that the EU's global influence is on a par with existing or emerging superpowers. It does, however, rest on an acknowledgement of the EU as a relevant actor at the global scene whose foreign policy affects citizens both within and beyond its borders.

Within the overall aim of achieving a clearer basis for a continuous discussion of the status of democracy in this domain, the contributions to this collection address the following questions:

(1) What is the significance of institutional changes for the principles and procedures of intergovernmental decision-making?
(2) If a move beyond intergovernmentalism has taken place, what kinds of competences and powers have been uploaded to the EU level?
(3) If a – putative – move beyond intergovernmentalism should be democratic, what sources of legitimation (if any) does the EU's foreign and security policy have to draw upon?

While some of the contributors mainly address the continued relevance of intergovernmentalism as a conceptual lens for the EU's foreign and security policy, others focus more explicitly on the question of democracy.

THE EU AND ITS FOREIGN AND SECURITY POLICY

The nature of the EU polity, as well as its democratic status, is contested. To some, democratic control and accountability are well taken care of through the traditional nation state channels, as the EU is essentially intergovernmental (Moravcsik 1998; Keohane *et al.* 2009). Others, while not necessarily questioning the intergovernmental core of the Union, consider that such indirect legitimation cannot bear the burden of democratic authorization (Lord 2011a). They link this to the complexity of the (intergovernmental) institutional networks. Others again argue that Europe has been transformed to such an extent that democracy must be anchored beyond the nation state (Bohman 2007; Eriksen 2009).

The literature on foreign and security policy has to a large extent developed in isolation from this broader debate. However, owing to its particularities, foreign and security policy actually constitutes an important test case. Foreign and security policy is considered alien to supranationalism, as its ultimate purpose is conventionally seen to be the protection of the 'national interest'. It is in a sense 'the ultimate bastion' of state sovereignty, and expectations that the EU's member states will move beyond intergovernmental processes of decision-making in this field have always been low. If a move beyond intergovernmentalism has taken place also here, this would be a strong indication of the EU becoming a polity in its own right. Yet, if foreign policy functions are simply 'uploaded' to the EU level without democratic control, the result would be a multi-level process of self-reinforcing executive dominance. In turn this would raise questions regarding the democratic anchoring of the polity as a whole.

This collection may contribute to the general debate regarding the conditions for democracy in Europe through its particular focus on foreign and security policy. Most importantly, however, in our endeavour to achieve a better understanding in empirical, conceptual and normative terms of what is at stake with regard to democracy and European foreign policy, we must draw on insights from the above debate. This is not least so as foreign policy in the EU may increasingly become less of a special case. It may be considered part of the general development of the 'executive power' of the European Union (Curtin and Egeberg 2008; Curtin 2009). Further, in order to develop sufficiently nuanced analytical tools as well as articulate critical standards for analysing and evaluating developments in this domain, insights from democratic theory as well as from studies of international relations are required. With more interaction between these 'worlds apart', our understanding would greatly improve.[3]

WHY BOTHER?

Given that foreign and security policy is only to varying degrees subject to democratic scrutiny at the national level, it may come as no surprise if the CFSP does not deliver well in democratic terms. However, there is no principled reason why foreign and security policy should not be subjected to democratic scrutiny. Foreign policy is different from domestic politics as law-making is less central, but it still has consequences for citizens. This 'structural difference' does not, then, exempt it from democratic scrutiny (Lord 2011b). The requirements of secrecy as well as of speed of decision-making that arise in this domain may be catered for as long as the principles and guidelines for secrecy themselves are publicly debated and regulated. When this is so, 'actors may operate, within given parameters, in secrecy without violating democratic norms'. (Eriksen 2011).

Still, is there really anything at stake if the CFSP does not live up to core democratic principles? After all, citizens have mostly been happy to leave foreign and security policy to the executives, assuming that they possess the required knowledge to act in the best interest of all. Foreign and security policy is seen mainly as an issue that interests the élites. It is only occasionally subject to great controversy, and rarely determines the outcome of elections. In the EU, the permissive consensus appears to persist with regard to this issue as public opinion is favourable to the idea of a common foreign policy for the EU (Peters 2011). But can we leave these matters in the hands of specialists and élites? References to the common good as well as the national interest are seductive, and yet without openness and public debate they may simply cover up for particular interests and values. If, as many observers seem to suggest, we are witnessing an expanding 'transnational bureaucracy', making decisions partly outside the public view and beyond the reach of national (and the European) parliaments, we cannot be sure that their decisions and assessments are in line with common interests.

CFSP AND GLOBAL TRANSFORMATIONS

The CFSP does not develop in a vacuum. New forms of governance emerge beyond the bounds of the (democratic) nation state. Problems and their solutions are defined and solved in a transnational and global context (Zürn 2005; Eriksen 2006). From the perspective of citizens, developments are ambivalent. On the one hand, the strengthening of international law and international institutions enhance citizens' scope of action. Developments in the direction of a civil society at the international level, involving transnational movements and non-governmental organizations, allow for transnational solidarity and common action (Bohman 1999; Held and Koenig–Archibugi 2005). Most importantly, they enhance citizens' rights at the expense of the sovereign state. According to Hauke Brunkhorst (2011), a legal revolution has taken place since the end of the Second World War:

> The old rule of equal sovereignty of states became the 'sovereign equality' *under* international law [...]. Individual human beings became subject to international law, democracy became an emerging right or a legal principle that is valid also against sovereign states, and the right to have rights, which Arendt missed in the 1940s, is now a legal norm that binds the international community. (Brunkhorst 2011: 12; emphasis original)

The point is not that these are always respected, but rather that when they are not overheld actors break the law.

However, the rise of a global regime of rights also gives rise to a fundamental dilemma. Although rights have been strengthened, the question is whether these are rights that citizens have given to themselves. Unless rights are subject to democratic authorization, they are ultimately part of a process of juridification. It is judges, then, rather than citizens or their representatives, who hold the key to power.

The European Union is often described as an engine of such global transformations. According to its Security Strategy it aims to develop a rule-based international order, stronger international society and well-functioning international institutions (Council of the European Union 2003). The United Nations is identified as the cornerstone of global order and the EU includes a human rights clause in all its international agreements. Insofar as the CFSP has acted as an agent for transformation of the international order, in favour of stronger cosmopolitan law, it may be seen as part of the wave of post-national 'good' governance (Brunkhorst 2011: 13; see also Eriksen 2006; Sjursen 2006). However, even 'good governance' is not democratic. As such it represents 'an accelerating process of a global *original accumulation of power beyond national and representative government*'. (Brunkhorst 2011: 14 [emphasis original]; Eriksen 2011). We may ask, then, whether the CFSP represents such post-national governance without democratic government. If this is so, it may embody a similar tension, as a promoter of rights that rests on uncertain democratic grounds.

Without solid grounding in democratic procedures we have fewer tools at our disposal to ensure that post-national governance does not turn from 'good' to 'bad' (Brunkhorst 2011). Against the backdrop of the 'war against terror' and the global financial crisis, as well as the rise of new powers – some with scant consideration for human rights – this may be a particular source of concern.

On the other hand, foreign and security policy is perhaps no longer an issue that citizens and parliaments are willing to blindly put in the hands of the executive. The permissive consensus may become less so. This may also be the case with regard to the CFSP, if it bows to the considerable structural pressure for it to abandon its Kantian stance and position itself in accordance with what many consider the emergence of a new balance of power.

THE ARGUMENTS MADE

The contributions to this collection must be seen as a first attempt at reorienting studies of European foreign and security policy towards the question of democracy. The hope is to provoke further analysis and debate regarding this topic.

In the first contribution I disentangle the key elements of democratic intergovernmentalism and assess its empirical status. I argue that in order for the CFSP to live up to core democratic requirements a reconstitutionalization of foreign and security policy would be required. Further pursuing the question of intergovernmentalism, Ana Juncos and Karolina Pomorska examine the role of officials from the working groups and the Council Secretariat in EU foreign policy. Owing to processes of socialization, the concept of intergovernmentalism does not adequately capture policy-making within these institutions. Federica Bicchi has studied the exchange of information across national and institutional boundaries within the EU – institutionalized in the so-called Correspondance Européenne (COREU) network. She finds that a community of practice has developed in which the red lines of the intergovernmental arena are crossed on a daily basis. While the first three contributions highlight departures from core principles of intergovernmentalism, and thus imply a need to address the question of democracy, Christopher Lord goes a long way towards claiming that even if the CFSP were purely intergovernmental there would be a need for direct legitimation at the EU level. He revisits the question of democratic control in foreign and security policy in general, as well as in the specific institutional context of the CFSP. Jutta Joachim and Matthias Dembinski suggest that we need to expand the actor focus in order to understand the CFSP. They find that non-governmental organizations were important in shaping the EU's code of conduct on arms exports. While Joachim and Dembinski advocate a governance perspective on the CFSP, Erik Oddvar Eriksen problematizes governance from the viewpoint of democracy. Discussing the role of expertise in EU security policy, he highlights the democratic pitfalls of the ambition of a comprehensive security strategy that blurs the boundaries between different forms of expertise as well as the separation of powers of the democratic Rechtsstat. He also stresses that factual knowledge in this domain is infused with values, hence problematizing the growing role of expertise in security policy. Finally, in the last contribution, Ben Tonra raises the question of identity and democracy. The weaknesses in the democratic legitimacy underpinning EU foreign and security policy, he argues, are in part a function of poor narrative construction in Europe. This fails to create a sense of ownership over the international actions of the Union.

Biographical note: Helene Sjursen is Professor at ARENA – Centre for European Studies, University of Oslo, Norway.

ACKNOWLEDGEMENTS

I wish to record special thanks to Michael Smith of Loughborough University for his important input and advice in the preparation of this collection. I also wish to thank Kathinka Louise Rinvik and Hanna Karv for research assistance and Erik Oddvar Eriksen for comments and advice. Many thanks are also due to the participants at the ARENA Workshop 'Simply uploading executive power? Democracy and the Common Foreign and Security Policy of the European Union', Oslo, 7–8 October 2010. This collection is a contribution to the Eurotrans project financed by the Norwegian Research Council. Financial support from the Norwegian Ministry of Foreign Affairs is also gratefully acknowledged.

NOTES

1 Federal Constitutional Court's Judgment (GCC) (30 June 2009), 2 BvE 2/08 vom 30.6.2009, para 211, available at http://www.bverfg.de/entscheidungen/es20090 630_2bve000208en.html (accessed 21 September 2011).
2 See, for example, Tonra (2003); Duke and Vanhoonacker (2006); Juncos and Reynolds (2007); Christiansen and Vanhoonacker (2008); Howorth (2010).
3 Amongst the many relevant works are Bohman (1999); Majone (2005); Pollack (2003); Eriksen (2009); Keohane *et al.* (2009); Brunkhorst (2011); Forst and Schmalz-Bruns (2011); Fossum and Menéndez (2011); as well as Eriksen (2011) and Lord (2011).

REFERENCES

Allen, D. (1998) 'Who speaks for Europe? The search for an effective and coherent external policy', in J. Peterson and H. Sjursen (eds), *A Common Foreign Policy for Europe?*, London: Routledge, pp. 42–58.
Allen, D. and Smith, M. (1990) 'Western Europe's presence in the contemporary international arena', *Review of International Studies* 16: 19–37.
Bohman, J. (1999) 'International regimes and democratic governance: political equality and influence in global institutions', *International Affairs* 75(3): 499–513.
Bohman, J. (2007) *Democracy across Borders: From Dêmos to Dêmoi*, Cambridge, MA: MIT Press.
Brunkhorst, H. (2011) 'Cosmopolitanism and democratic freedom', *RECON Online Working Paper 2011/09*, Oslo: ARENA, available at http://www.reconproject.eu/ main.php/RECON_wp_1109.pdf?fileitem=5456462 (accessed 21 September 2011).

Christiansen, T. and Vanhoonacker, S. (2008) 'At a critical juncture? Change and continuity in the institutional development of the Council Secretariat', *West European Politics* 31(4): 751–70.

Council of the European Union (2003), 'A secure Europe in a better world: European Security Strategy', Brussels, 12 December.

Crum, B. (2006) 'Parliamentarization of the CFSP through informal institution-making? The fifth European Parliament and the EU High Representative', *Journal of European Public Policy* 13(3): 383–401.

Curtin, D. (2009) *Executive Power of the European Union: Law, Practices and the Living Constitution*, Oxford: Oxford University Press.

Curtin, D. and Egeberg, M. (2008) 'Tradition and innovation: Europe's accumulated executive order', *West European Politics* 31(4): 639–61.

Duchêne, F. (1972) 'Europe's role in world peace', in R. Mayne (ed.), *Europe Tomorrow: Sixteen Europeans Look Ahead*, London: Fontana, pp. 32–47.

Duke, S. and Vanhoonacker, S. (2006) 'Administrative governance and CFSP', in H.C.H. Hofmann and A.H. Türk (eds), *EU Administrative Governance*, Cheltenham: Edward Elgar, pp. 31–55.

Eriksen, E.O. (2006) 'The EU: a cosmopolitan polity?,' *Journal of European Public Policy* 13(2): 252–69.

Eriksen, E.O. (2009) *The Unfinished Democratization of Europe*, Oxford: Oxford University Press.

Eriksen, E.O. (2011) 'Governance between expertise and democracy: the case of European security', *Journal of European Public Policy* 18(8): 1169–89.

Forst, R. and Schmalz-Bruns, R. (2011) 'Political legitimacy and democracy in transnational perspective', *RECON Report No. 13*, Oslo: ARENA.

Fossum, J.E. and Menéndez, A.J. (2011) *The Constitution's Gift*, Lanham, MD: Rowman and Littlefield.

Galtung, J. (1973) *The European Community: A Superpower in the Making*, Sydney: Allen and Unwin.

Held, D. and Koenig-Archibugi, M. (eds) (2005) *Global Governance and Public Accountability*, Oxford: Blackwell.

Hill, C. (1990) 'European foreign policy: power bloc, civilian model – or flop?', in R. Rummel (ed.), *The Evolution of an International Actor: Western Europe's New Assertiveness*, Boulder, CO: Westview Press, pp. 31–55.

Howorth, J. (2010) 'The Political and Security Committee: a case study in "supranational inter-governmentalism"', *Les Cahiers europeens de Sciences Po*, No. 01/2010, Paris: Centre d'études européennes at Sciences Po, available at http://www.cee.sciences-po.fr/erpa/docs/wp_2010_1.pdf (accessed 21 September2011).

Juncos, A.E. and Reynolds, C. (2007) 'The Political and Security Committee: governing in the shadow', *European Foreign Affairs Review* 12: 127–47.

Keohane, R., Macedo, S. and Moravcsik, A. (2009) 'Democracy-enhancing multilateralism', *International Organization* 63: 1–31.

Lord, C. (2011a) 'Polecats, lions, and foxes: coasian bargaining theory and attempts to legitimate the Union as a constrained form of political power', *European Political Science Review* 3(1): 83–102.

Lord, C. (2011b) 'The political theory and practice of Parliamentary participation in the Common Security and Defence Policy', *Journal of European Public Policy* 18(8): 1133–50.

Majone, G. (2005) *Dilemmas of European Integration: The Ambiguities and Pitfalls of Integration by Stealth*, Oxford: Oxford University Press.

McCormick, J. (2007) *The European Superpower*, New York: Palgrave Macmillan.

Moravcsik, A. (1998) *The Choice for Europe: Social Purpose and State Power from Messina to Maastricht*, London: University College London Press.

Peters, D. (2011) 'A divided Union? Public opinion and the EU's Common Foreign, Security and defence Policy', *RECON Online Working Paper 2011/19*, Oslo: ARENA, available at http://www.reconproject.eu/main.php/RECON_wp_1119. pdf?fileitem=5456481 (accessed 21 September 2011)

Pollack, M.A. (2003) *The Engines of European Integration: Delegation, Agency and Agenda Setting in the EU*, Oxford: Oxford University Press.

Sjøstedt, G. (1977) *The External Role of the European Community*, Farnborough: Saxon House.

Sjursen, H. (2006) 'What kind of power?', *Journal of European Public Policy* 13(2): 169–81.

Smith, K.E. (2000) 'The end of civilian power EU: a welcome demise or cause for concern?', *International Spectator* 35(2): 11–28.

Thym, D. (2006) 'Beyond Parliament's reach? The role of the European Parliament in the CFSP', *European Foreign Affairs Review* 11: 109–27.

Tonra, B. (2003) 'Constructing the Common Foreign and Security Policy: the utility of a cognitive approach', *Journal of Common Market Studies* 42(4): 731–56.

Wagner, W. (2006) 'The democratic control of military power in Europe', *Journal of European Public Policy* 13(2): 200–16.

Zielonka, J. (2006) *Europe as Empire: The Nature of the Enlarged European Union*, Oxford: Oxford University Press.

Zürn, M. (2005) 'Global governance and communicative action', in D. Held and M. Koenig-Archibugi (eds), *Global Governance and Public Accountability*, Oxford: Blackwell Publishing, pp. 136–63.

Not so intergovernmental after all? On democracy and integration in European Foreign and Security Policy

Helene Sjursen

ABSTRACT   The status of democracy in European foreign and security policy is increasingly questioned. In order to identify if there is something at the European Union (EU) level that requires legitimation, we need to establish whether there has been a move beyond intergovernmentalism. In this contribution an analytical scheme that makes it possible to identify such a move and its putative democratic implications is developed. Four constituent pillars of intergovernmentalism are identified and discussed. These pertain to actors, decision-making procedures, the scope of delegated powers and the *raison d'être* of the intergovernmental endeavour. These pillars constitute necessary requirements if intergovernmentalism is to be democratic. Developments within the Common Foreign and Security Policy (CFSP) are assessed with reference to this analytical scheme, with a view to identify whether, when and where a move beyond intergovernmentalism has created a democratic dilemma.

What is the status of democracy in the field of European foreign, security and defence policy? In order to answer this question it is necessary to clarify the depth and form of integration in this policy field. It is only when we know what kind of polity we are faced with – what power(s) it has – that it is possible to identify any putative democratic deficit at the European level. Whenever there are relations of domination there is a requirement for democratic forms of rule under modern conditions.

According to key European foreign-policy-makers, such as France's Prime Minister François Fillon and his Spanish counterpart Foreign Minister Miguel Moratinos, it is the member states that decide on European foreign and security policy (European Parliament 2010). In this intergovernmental conception of the Common Foreign and Security Policy (CFSP), power and authority lie exclusively at the national level. It is implied that national institutions and procedures are sufficient to take care of democratic concerns. But can national governments and national foreign ministers be held accountable for what they do in the context of CFSP and the Common Security and Defence Policy (CSDP)?

And further, is it possible to trace the decisions made in the CFSP and CSDP back to a democratic mandate given by citizens within each member state? In order to identify whether there is something at the European Union (EU) level that needs legitimation, we need to establish whether a move beyond inter-governmentalism has taken place. In this contribution I suggest an analytical framework that makes it possible to identify such a move, as well as its putative democratic implications.

Recent research points towards a more complex institutional structure and decision-making process than that implied by the concept of intergovernmental co-operation. However, these findings are rarely discussed from the perspective of democracy. Rather, efficiency tends to be the underlying concern in analyses of institutions and decision-making in the CFSP. If a departure from inter-governmentalism has taken place, the democratic chain of delegation is prob-ably broken. If this is so, there is something at the EU level that would require legitimation. However, it may also be that the range of policy-making and the many hands involved in European foreign and security policy make the intergovernmental model of delegatory control obsolete, even if the CFSP formally retains its intergovernmental character.

First, however, it is necessary to clarify what is meant by democracy. I start out by briefly highlighting what may be considered core democratic requirements. In the second part of the paper a conception of intergovernmentalism that is consistent with these requirements is outlined. Further, indicators of a departure from intergovernmentalism are suggested. Having thus laid out the analytical framework, I then provide some examples in the third part of what it would take to corroborate a hypothesis of a move beyond intergovernmentalism in the CFSP/CSDP. To what extent and in what ways (if at all) has intergovern-mentalism been modified? Before concluding, I return (in the fourth part) to the question of democracy.

DEMOCRACY IN EUROPEAN FOREIGN AND SECURITY POLICY

If one is to examine whether or not there are any reasons to raise the issue of democracy with regard to the EU's foreign and security policy, it is necessary first to specify what is meant by democracy. What are core democratic require-ments, and what should we look for in order to find out if European foreign and security policy satisfies these requirements?

At a principled level, democracy implies that citizens should be able to govern themselves through law and politics; that is, a democratic system must be consist-ent with the requirements of *autonomy* and *accountability*. These principles, which are at the core of modern ideas of democracy, are identifiable in most the-ories, and may thus be seen to constitute a 'democratic minimum' (Eriksen 2009; cp. Dahl 1989; Rawls 1993; Pettit 1997). They are an explicit part of Habermas' discourse-theoretical model of deliberative democracy (Habermas 1996). From this perspective it is the democratic procedure that is conceived of as key. This perspective may be seen to seek to bridge republican and liberal conceptions of democracy. The autonomy requirement pertains to the ability of those affected by laws also to be their authors: '[i]ntrinsic to this criterion is the possibility of the authorised bodies of decision-making to react adequately on public support to determine the development of the political community in such a way that the citizens can be seen to act upon themselves' (Eriksen 2009: 36). When investigating to what extent this principle is properly respected, key questions then are: 'who decides – and on what issues?'. In order to find out whether it is possible to trace decisions back to the authorization given by citizens, we need to map where and how decisions are made. Further important questions pertain to whether or not, and in what ways, there are institutions and procedures in place that allow for the openness, access to information and debate that would make it possible for citizens to have an informed opinion (Held 2006: 262–3).

As for accountability, the issue is whether those who decide can be held responsible for their decisions. The key, in other words, is whether citizens can (or cannot) impose sanctions on those in power:

> Accountability designates a relationship wherein obligatory questions are posed and qualified answers required. It speaks to a justificatory process that rests on a reason-giving practice, wherein the decision-makers can be held responsible to the citizenry, and by which, in the last resort, it is possible to dismiss incompetent rulers. (Eriksen 2009: 36; see also Bovens *et al.* 2010)

In this context we must ask not only *who* is held responsible, but also to whom, and regarding which issues? What rights and resources do citizens have in this regard?

By taking the two principles of accountability and autonomy as a starting point, the net is cast wider than by previous studies on democracy and CFSP. The focus in these studies is on the role and influence of the European Parliament (EP) (Diedrichs 2004; Barbé 2004; Bono 2006; Thym 2006; Peters *et al.* 2008). However, simply investigating the powers of the EP does not tell us much about the status of democracy in the CFSP. The relevance and importance of the EP must be assessed in the context of the institutional set-up as a whole. It is only once we have established whether there is something to legitimize at the EU level in the first place that the powers (or lack of such) of the EP can function as an indicator of the status of democracy. So far, the literature on the EP has treated this issue too lightly. In order to address this, we need an analytical framework that disentangles the various components of intergovernmentalism and explicates how such a system, in which there is no direct link between the citizens and the decision-makers, can be consistent with the requirements of autonomy and accountability.

UNPACKING THE INTERGOVERNMENTAL MODEL OF DELEGATORY CONTROL

Intergovernmentalism is a system akin to a contract (Frankenberg 2000) or international treaty. A contract (or treaty) is signed between sovereign parties. This means that each state retains jurisdiction within its own territory and remains free to organize its institutions and policy processes according to its own preferences. The powers of the central public authority, in this case the EU, are closely limited. It is obligated to observe the rights and competences of each member government. Beyond this, such contracts are 'remarkably silent on the integration issue and further presuppose the question of legitimate authority as being answered elsewhere' (Frankenberg 2000: 260). This is because democratic legitimacy is indirect, derived from the political systems of the signatory (nation) states. Various mechanisms, such as the delegation of power and the right to veto, as well as that of withdrawal, are in place in order to ensure that the principles of autonomy and accountability may be taken care of at the national level (Arrow 1985; Pollack 2003; Eriksen and Fossum 2011).

Whether such a system can remain democratic has been problematized (Lord 2011a; see also Lord 2011b). And, as references abound to 'supranational intergovernmentalism', 'Brussels-based intergovernmentalism', 'deliberative intergovernmentalism' and the like, this question becomes even more pertinent (Allen 1998; Howorth 2001; Puetter 2003; Juncos and Pomorska 2006; Juncos and Reynolds 2007; Howorth 2010). How much integration can intergovernmentalism take before it stops being intergovernmental? Do all these variants of intergovernmentalism remain consistent with the principles of autonomy and accountability?

In order to investigate these questions empirically, the concept of intergovernmentalism must be further unpacked, and the way in which the core principles of accountability and autonomy are institutionalized clarified. Indicators of what might be seen as departures from the delegatory model of control may then be specified.

Four constituent pillars of democratic intergovernmentalism

Drawing on the above conceptions of intergovernmentalism (Moravcsik 1998; Majone 2001; Pollack 2003), democratic intergovernmentalism may be seen to institutionalize the principles of accountability and autonomy through the means of four constituent pillars. They work as constraints on the powers of the intergovernmental 'unit'. The four pillars or premises concern: (1) the nature of the actors involved in making decisions; (2) the procedures through which decisions are made; (3) the scope and type of powers that are delegated; and (4) the *raison d'être* of the co-operative endeavour. These pillars are to some extent interdependent. However, by making an analytical distinction between them, a more nuanced and detailed empirical analysis becomes possible. Each of these may be challenged separately (or of course in parallel). This means that while the assumption is that all four are necessary premises in order for the intergovernmental model of delegatory control to be democratic, not all may be required in order to ensure the smooth running of the system.

The first premise indicates that only sovereign states can be actors with decision-making powers in an intergovernmental system. The establishment of supranational institutions with a self-standing constitutional basis would represent a departure from intergovernmentalism. However, one can also imagine other actors representing interests and perspectives beyond the member states achieving decision-shaping powers. If non-governmental organizations, private corporations, agencies or institutions of some kind wield influence, this would also challenge this first premise of the intergovernmental edifice. Even if these various actors were not able to lay down the law to member states, they might influence decisions.

The second premise concerns the decision-making procedure. The right of each member state to veto any decision with which it disagrees is a cornerstone of an intergovernmental system. Abandoning this and introducing decision-making by some form of majority vote would be a clear indication of a departure from intergovernmental principles. However, the veto power of the contracting parties might also be constrained in less formal ways. One can imagine, for example, the hands of the contracting parties being tied owing to constraints on time. (Normative) expectations of non-use of the veto might also develop for other reasons. Finally, it might also be that, owing to differences in power and authority, the ability to block a decision is more real for some than for others.

The third premise concerns the idea that powers are only delegated, and that the member states may revoke or renegotiate them. It seems implicit in this premise that the delegated tasks should be concrete and precisely delimited. It would otherwise be difficult to ensure national control, or indeed to maintain control and to bring an issue back into the 'national fold'. If the delegated powers are wide in scope it might be difficult to control and withdraw them. Also, if delegated powers are associated with a degree of discretion, this changes the sense in which powers are simply delegated. There might also be a *de facto* difference between the freedoms of action of different member states in this regard. Some, more powerful, states might more easily be able to revoke delegated powers than others.

The fourth premise concerns the purpose or *raison d'être* of intergovernmental co-operation. An intergovernmental system is established to serve the member states and to assist them in forwarding, or protecting, their preferences and values. An intergovernmental unit infused with interests or values of its own would represent a departure from the fourth pillar. Such a purpose might in turn constrain the ability of member states freely to define their policies in accordance with their own preferences.

What does existing knowledge regarding the institutions and decision-making procedures within CFSP/CSDP tell us about the status of these four constitutional pillars? To what extent is the hypothesis that a move beyond intergovernmentalism has taken place plausible?

BEYOND INTERGOVERNMENTALISM?

Who decides? The fragmentation of the state administrative apparatus

In formal terms, the answer to the above question is simple, and in line with the first premise of intergovernmentalism: it is the member states that decide in EU foreign and security policy. That is, decisions are taken by the foreign ministers of all the member states in the Foreign Affairs Committee (FAC), or by the heads of state and government in the European Council. However, the range of actors involved in CFSP/CSDP is much wider than this. As Joachim and Dembinski (2011) suggest, non-governmental organizations (NGOs) as well as private corporations influence decision-making processes. Most important in this regard, however, are the permanent intergovernmental institutions in Brussels. While they were established in order to facilitate decision-making in the FAC or European Council, they have gained considerable autonomy. It is because of their role, not because of non-state actors or supranational institutions, that the first premise of intergovernmentalism, that states are the only actors in EU foreign policy, is being undermined.

At the centre of the intergovernmental institutional nexus is the Political and Security Committee (PSC). Composed of national ambassadors permanently based in Brussels, it has been described as the 'linchpin' of the system of foreign and security policy (Duke 2004) and as the 'executive board' of the CFSP (Thym 2011). Its mandate is to 'monitor the international situation and contribute to the definition of policies' (Art. 38.1 TEU). The PSC also delivers opinions to the Council and exercises political control over and strategic direction of crisis-management operations. Also of importance are the various working groups examined in more detail by Juncos and Pomorska (2011), as well as the EU Military Committee (EUMC) and the Committee for Civilian Aspects of Crisis Management (CIVCOM). In addition, the High Representative and the newly established European External Action Service (EEAS) are important institutions within the CFSP.

Research suggests that, over time, these institutions have gained considerable autonomy from the governments that they are meant to serve (Tonra 2000, 2003; Meyer 2006; Vanhoonacker *et al.* 2010). They do not merely fulfil support functions for the FAC, or act as co-ordinating mechanisms for the member states. Already in 2006, Duke and Vanhoonacker found in their study of these Brussels-based institutions that the 'question whether the administrative level matters in the foreign policy field should definitely be answered affirmatively' (2006: 380). As already noted, the PSC is particularly important in this regard. It is here that common positions are identified and the methods to realize them are developed. Juncos and Reynolds (2007) have described the PSC as *governing in the shadow.* Howorth (2010) refers to the PSC as the 'script writer' for the CFSP, in the sense that its members 'come up with policies, missions and operations for the EU which will allow it to demonstrate both its usefulness and its importance' (Howorth 2010: 18).

These observations of a shift in decision-making power from national capitals to the institutional machinery in Brussels suggest a strengthening of the executive branch. However, they also suggest a fragmentation of the executive power of national governments, as the agents of national governments in Brussels have a hand on the steering wheel. I return to the first point in the section on democracy. It should be noted here too, however, that it makes it more difficult to identify who really decides.

'Fuzziness' concerning where responsibility actually lies is reinforced by the difficulty in establishing clear distinctions between foreign and security policy on the one hand and all other aspects of EU global activities on the other (Smith 2004: 7-8). While (in principle) the former are supposed to be under the control of national governments, the latter are subject to supranational procedures. In practice, it is not as simple as this, as a number of issues are of so-called mixed competence. This has led to double-headed missions and ad hoc solutions in which the Commission and representatives of the Council have both been involved. This difficulty has resulted in turf war and institutional competition and as such is usually addressed as a challenge to the objective of a coherent foreign policy (Smith 2001). However, it also raises questions regarding democracy, as it is not possible, with regard to such issues, to claim unequivocally that national governments decide in European foreign and security policy.

Apart from those issues that transgress the established borders of the 'CFSP/ CSDP proper', the roles and influence of the supranational institutions are limited. As already noted, the main challenge to the first premise of intergovern-mentalism comes from within the intergovernmental structures. The transform-ation of the organization of the whole field of foreign and security policy which will follow from the Lisbon Treaty and the establishment of the European External Action Service promise to reinforce these tendencies. Amongst other things, the logic of recruitment contrasts with intergovernmental principles, as 60 per cent of staff in the EEAS are permanent and all staff are appointed 'on merit' rather than on geographical/national origin. In other words, the autonomy of the Brussels-based machinery developed prior to Lisbon might in the future be further reinforced. The difficulties of monitoring the borders between the intergovernmental and supranational strands of the EU's role in the world also remain, or are perhaps even reinforced. Supranationalism and intergovernmentalism now live together under the same roof. This coexistence starts with the High Representative, whose authority is derived from the member states, and who is also part of the Commission. As for the EEAS, it exists to assist her, and thus must face this distinction in its daily activities. Again, the question of 'who decides' is partly fudged.

What, then, of the second basic premise of intergovernmentalism? How real is the right of member states to veto decisions with which they disagree?

Sidestepping the veto

Many studies point to significant changes to the way in which policy is made within the institutions dealing with foreign and security policy (Tonra 2003; Meyer 2006; Vanhoonacker *et al.* 2010). Juncos and Pomorska (1996) and Juncos and Reynolds (2007) find strong evidence of compliance with specific codes of conduct referred to as 'consensus building' as well as with the often-mentioned reflex of co-ordination. Thus, they echo much of what Simon

Nuttall argued (Nuttall 2000). Howorth finds that 'a significant measure of socialization ensures that the dominant mode of interaction is consensus-seeking rather than bargaining around fixed national positions' (Howorth 2010: 16).

However, this literature is often shrouded in a certain conceptual and theoretical vagueness, which makes it difficult to know precisely what has changed, and what it might tell us about the status of intergovernmentalism and the member states' right to veto. One important aspect to the claim of socialization is that the positions of the member states over time are becoming more similar. However, the observation that perspectives or policy-positions of member states are becoming more alike does not necessarily signify that the CFSP is no longer intergovernmental. Such transformations may decrease the likelihood of the use of the veto and hence facilitate policy-making, but this is still a different matter. Likewise, the observations made regarding actors as 'consensus-seeking' may be compatible with the right to veto. As consensus-seeking implies that all must agree to a decision (or at least agree not to overtly disagree), such consensus-seeking may well take place 'in the shadow of the veto'.

On the other hand, insofar as this literature represents a critique of rational-choice, intergovernmentalist assumptions of actors' preferences as exogenous and of the outcome of decisions as the lowest common denominator of such predefined preferences, it does indirectly question the centrality of the veto. The argument is that, rather than being exogenous to the process of decision-making, preferences are shaped through a collective, cross-border decision-making process. If member states routinely, as the reflex of co-ordination suggests, postpone defining their preferences on foreign policy issues until they have spoken to their European partners, or if they define their position in a process of exchange with their partners, this could mean that the veto is no longer relevant, even though it does not question its existence.

This sense of the veto as a less central element in decision-making also emerges from the fact that member states often do not have clearly defined preferences. In such cases they often simply go along with the collective position (Juncos and Reynolds 2007; Howorth 2010: 17–18). However, as it is then not a matter of member states *changing* positions, but simply of *developing* a position, neither these observations, nor those of a collective, cross-border decision-making process, are irreconcilable with the right to veto. We can only really claim that this right is challenged if we find that states refrain from using it. This question is addressed more directly in a study of the EU's work on preparing its positions and policies during the negotiations concerning the International Labour Organization's (ILO) Maritime Convention. The authors find that in this case member states were willing to forego their right to veto in order to develop a common policy (Riddervold and Sjursen forthcoming, 2012). This was also true for states with strong economic interests that ran counter to the proposed common positions. While this is not a classic CFSP issue, it is an example of EU member states deliberately choosing to act together rather than separately in an international setting. As such, it is certainly an issue of foreign policy (Jørgensen 2009) and it constitutes a challenge to the assumption that a change in the norms that guide decision-making – away from a practice where the threat of a veto is constantly present – is unrealistic.

Several observations of interaction within the PSC point in this same direction. Participants here describe processes in which they routinely succeed in convincing state representatives to change from their initial position:

> If we have a wave of consensus and you are the only obstacle, then you have to have exceptionally good arguments to turn the tide. Sometimes, colleagues have to say: 'Yes I understand everybody else, and I would love to agree but I simply have to call home.' Then everybody will agree to let him/her call home. Very, very often, I would say, it is also the case that the colleague will come back and say: 'Yes, OK, we agree!' (quoted in Howorth 2010: 16).

Likewise, Christoph Meyer finds that agreement has been achieved 'even in areas where national strategic norms would initially indicate incompatibility' (Meyer 2006: 136).

The veto, or its shadow, remains, even though it is often sidestepped. Most importantly, however, and contrary to conventional wisdom, there are several examples of member states changing their initial position, rather than vetoing a decision, for the sake of the 'common good'. While there are not yet sufficient systematic empirical studies to claim that these examples represent a trend, they are significant enough to suggest that the ground below the feet of the veto is not entirely solid. Most importantly, they underline the difficulty of disaggregating decisions and tracing them back to individual foreign ministers and their governments, which in turn raises questions regarding democratic accountability.

Scope and type of competences

The third premise of intergovernmentalism concerns the delegation of power and the right of member states to revoke it – or to renegotiate its terms. There is little to draw on in terms of actual practice with regard to this premise. We do not know what would happen if a state sought to withdraw powers that had been delegated, as no one has sought to do so. Thus, a different kind of analysis is required. I focus on what may be considered the best interpretation of the idea of the delegation of power and look at the extent to which this fits the formal arrangements that are in place. On this basis, some questions arise.

First, rather than delegating a limited set of tasks, the Treaties indicate a general delegation of competence in all matters relating to foreign policy and the Union's security, as well as identifying the aim of a common defence. Certainly, this general delegation is limited by the fact that within this overall frame, each decision to act is made by the member states 'acting unanimously' (Art.11.1-2). Nevertheless, this generalized delegation raises some doubts with regard to the reality of the right to revoke powers that have already been delegated. Presumably it is easier to 'take back' into the national fold specific tasks that are limited in time. There is a sense of permanence to the delegation of general competence, which is reinforced by the establishment of instruments and capabilities at the EU level. As already discussed, the EU is developing its own apparatus of external representation (via the EEAS). It may also deploy troops, using the concept of the battle group, amongst others, and it may sign treaties, as it has obtained legal personality in the Lisbon Treaty. This permanent ability to act within what may be seen as core dimensions of foreign and security policy seems to be at odds with the temporariness associated with delegation.

While doubts are often raised with regard to the prospects for further expansion of tasks at the EU level, there are no expectations of a reduction. The assumption seems to be that a decision to delegate is rather definite. In fact, observers even point to a 'ratchet effect' in the way the CFSP has been designed in the Treaties: 'Right from the beginning, each constitutive report contained within it the seeds of its successor' (Hill 1993: 275). Also daily decision-making processes are often considered to have a cumulative effect. As Nuttall argues, the accumulation of previous stances on foreign-policy issues provides a common framework for action and decision (Nuttall 2000; see also Smith 2004: 141). These observations not only underline the definitive nature of the act of delegation but also suggest that it carries with it the potential for further commitments. The practice is different from that entailed by the idea of powers which are delegated and which may subsequently be withdrawn. Incidentally, on this issue, the right to veto might actually have adverse effects: if a state wants to dismantle this system, it would in all likelihood require the support of all the member states, or it would mean that the state in question leaves the EU altogether.

Finally, and perhaps most importantly, this generalized delegation opens zones, or pockets, of discretion for the institutions at the EU level. Amongst other things, it widens the scope of initiatives that may be taken by the now semi-autonomous institutions and bodies in Brussels, such as the EEAS and the PSC. In their search for possible common policies, they are authorized to look along the entire spectrum from foreign policy to defence. Further, within the scope of a particular task, there may be considerable room for discretion. This is particularly so with regard to the CSDP and military missions where the powers delegated to the PSC are considerable, although in foreign policy more generally there is also room for autonomous action (Art. 38(2) TEU).

The fragmentation of European foreign and security policy is also notable when this premise of intergovernmentalism is analysed. Although member states maintain their legal competences in all matters of foreign and security policy, such competences are not exclusive to them. Two parallel but interwoven systems of foreign policy are emerging – that of the nation states and that of the EU.

European interests and values

The fourth and final premise of intergovernmentalism identified in the analytical framework concerns the purpose, or *raison d'être*, of the intergovernmental endeavour.

An intergovernmental entity is there to serve the member states, to assist them in solving concrete problems, to ensure the protection of their interests and values and to enforce their preferences. However, in the case of the EU, there has been a conscious effort to go beyond this, to define *European* interests, as well as *European* values. The most coherent definition of these interests and values may be found in the European Security Strategy, adopted by the European Council in December 2003. The Security Strategy 'established principles and set clear objectives for advancing the EU's security interests based on our core values' (Council of the European Union 2008). It set out three strategic objectives for European security: tackling key threats, building security in our neighborhood and promoting an international order based on effective multilateralism (Council of the European Union 2003). The conception of the EU as an actor with a purpose of its own, beyond that of serving the interests and preferences of the member states, also comes through in the Treaty texts. Thus, one may read in the Lisbon Treaty: '*the Union* shall ... assert *its identity* on the international scene' (Title I, art. 2; emphasis added). This, then, seems to constitute a departure from the fourth premise of intergovernmentalism.

Through such definitions of the interests and values of the EU, constraints are also put on the actions of individual member states. These are partly of a legal nature. The member states are, according to Article 11(2) of the Treaty of Lisbon, legally bound to support the Union's foreign and security policy 'actively and unreservedly in a spirit of loyalty and mutual solidarity'. In fact, according to Cremona, 'the most important element of the Treaty of Lisbon from the perspective of foreign policy coherence is the clear external mandate given to the Union as a whole in both substantive and instrumental terms' (Cremona 2008: 35). However, equally important is the binding force of norms and institutions established prior to the Lisbon Treaty. In fact, despite the well-known solo initiatives of some of the EU's member states in situations of crisis, it is increasingly difficult for member states to escape expectations of consistency between national foreign policy and the foreign policy positions of the EU (Sjursen 2003).

The development of an overarching normative frame constrains, in turn, the member states' ability freely to define national foreign and security policy, as the idea of intergovernmentalism assumes they should. Participation in the CFSP has led to a reorientation of the foreign policies of member states. Alfred Pijpers noted this already in 1996 (Pijpers 1996: 252), as did Torreblanca with regard to Spain (Torreblanca 2001:11–12). Also, the largest member states, France, Germany and the United Kingdom, display evidence of such transformations as a result of membership of the CFSP (Aggestam 2004). The requirement to consult, under which national positions would have to be justified in a manner that makes it acceptable to all, might contribute to make member states seek a certain consistency between their claims and the underlying constitutive principles of the EU (Sjursen 2003).

The definition of a common purpose beyond the individual preferences and values of the member states is reinforced through the unity of the legal order, which was established with the Treaty of Lisbon. In discussions of the abolition of the pillar structure, the focus is most often on the limitations to this change, owing to the fact that the CFSP is still subject to specific rules and procedures (House of Commons 2008). However, with regard to the overall purpose of the CFSP, and the principles to which it is bound, the unity of the legal order does make a difference. With the abolition of the pillar structure the CFSP is subject to the same constitutional control standards as the rest of the EU. The Charter of Rights is binding for the EU as a whole, hence also for foreign, security and defence policy. This thus raises the stakes to some extent with regard to expectations of consistency, as it introduces an element of legal accountability. It remains the case, however, that the EU does not have formal mechanisms to sanction those who do not comply with the collectively agreed policy, or indeed with any of the constraints introduced in the Treaties.

A particular conception of European interests and values has been developed. Thus, we are some way towards the establishment of institutions devoted to the Union itself, rather than to the member states. This suggests that when the EU acts, it does so on behalf of something more than the mere sum of member states' interests; it does more than act on the delegated authority of the member states. What the EU does must be consistent with the Treaties and the overarching normative framework of the EU, not only with the interests of the member states. Further, the identification of such values impacts on the formulation of the member states' own foreign policies.

IMPLICATIONS FOR DEMOCRACY

While European foreign and security policy has not become supranational, it is equally problematic to claim that it remains intergovernmental. Several steps beyond the four premises of intergovernmentalism suggested in the analytical framework developed here have been taken. As a consequence, the ability of the CFSP/CSDP system to live up to the requirements of autonomy and accountability is under pressure.

A key challenge is to identify 'who decides'. It is often difficult to know, or predict, where responsibility for decisions actually lies. Foreign and security policy is made through interactions and exchanges between the executive branches of the member states. This makes it difficult to disaggregate decisions and trace them back to individual ministers or governments. Key actors are the representatives of the member states in Brussels, whose autonomy and room for discretion is considerable. Other actors, such as the supranational institutions and NGOs, also in some cases wield influence. More importantly, however, policy is shaped with reference to values and principles that are seen as particular to the Union, and not with exclusive reference to the interests and values of the member states. Often, states refrain from vetoing decisions, or change their position, in order to facilitate common policies.

Arguably, there is a democratizing and 'civilizing' element to this, as the requirement for national executives to justify their positions and actions is much more intense than in the traditional international setting (Keohane *et al.* 2009). The expectation that national governments justify their policies will probably be fortified by the legal obligations resulting from the unified legal framework established by the Lisbon Treaty. There are now some formal legal obligations, such as the Charter of Rights, to which governments must refer when justifying their policies, in addition to the overall normative ethos of CFSP. Nevertheless, these justifications of foreign policies take place between and among executives. To the extent that accountability plays a part, it is a matter of legal accountability (through national courts) and not accountability to elected representatives. Also, as mechanisms for ensuring compliance are not in place, those in power may simply 'talk the talk' and act regardless.

Consequently, this form of collective, cross-national decision-making seems difficult to reconcile with the principle that it should be possible to trace decisions back to a form of authorization by the citizens. Such authorization would probably require institutions and procedures beyond the individual nation states that would allow citizens access to information about what goes on amongst the executives and to have an informed opinion. Given that developments so far are the result mainly of informal practice, however, it is difficult to establish procedures that may compensate for their effects on citizens' status as authors of the policies. Also, there is a sense of contingency or haphazardness about which issues are brought outside the intergovernmental mode of decision-making, which makes it difficult to ensure proper channels and mechanisms of authorization. To the extent that there is a general pattern, it is that of segmented policy-making and the coexistence and overlapping of parallel systems of foreign policy. The institutions established in Brussels are part of the national executives, but their semi-autonomy contributes to a fragmentation of these same executives. The fragmentation of European foreign and security policy is also notable in that although member states maintain their legal competences in all matters of foreign and security policy, it is not exclusive to them. Incidentally, this fragmentation stands in contrast to the aspiration to coherence contained within the Lisbon Treaty.

There are of course exceptions. In the most dramatic international events or crises, it is much easier to trace the lines of authority back to national executives. Also, when it comes to implementation the EU must rely mostly on the national system. However, this does not solve the challenges involved in tracing those responsible and holding them to account.

As it is difficult to find out where decisions are actually made, it is also unclear who should be accountable. The EP has, through active pressure, gradually extended its influence (Barbé 2004; Maurer *et al.* 2005; Crum 2009). The general rule is, however, that it is only consulted on the main aspects and basic choices made in the field of foreign and security policy and is kept informed of how those policies evolve. With the establishment of the EEAS it has succeeded in strengthening its position a little further, as the High Representative is subject to Parliamentary questioning on the same basis as the Commissioners. Further, its role in deciding on the budget of the EEAS is important. And finally, its active involvement in the discussion on the entire set-up of the EEAS suggests that it may in future be a more influential actor. However, it is widely acknowledged that it neither authorizes decisions, nor is able to hold those that make decisions accountable (Bono 2006; Peters *et al.* 2008; Crum 2009). Moreover, the powers of national parliaments are limited owing to these very departures from the core premises of intergovernmentalism.

Simply strengthening the powers of the EP may, however, not be a sufficient solution to the democratic challenges of the CFSP. As already noted, it is the lack of clarity with regard to where authority and power actually lie that is the greatest challenge. What might be required, then, is a thorough (re-)constitutionalization of foreign and security policy, in order to clarify lines of authority and power. Simply increasing the powers of the EP would probably not solve the challenges involved unless it also brought with it a true supranationalization of foreign and security policy.

CONCLUSION

Peter Hain, representative of the British government to the European Convention, considers that '[i]f foreign policy is to enjoy legitimacy, there must be accountability through elected governments to national parliaments'.[1] Such a claim rests on the assumption that the CFSP is – and ought to remain – intergovernmental. However, the analysis conducted here suggests that something beyond intergovernmentalism has developed at the EU level and requires legitimation. It is difficult to see that this can be ensured through national procedures for accountability and authorization.

In order to reach this conclusion I have drawn on existing research on institutions and decision-making in the CFSP. The main contribution of this paper is to refocus the discussion on such issues towards the specific question of 'intergovernmentalism and beyond' and, in particular, to suggest how such a question may be approached. The take here is also different from the above institutional literature in that the onus is on establishing the actual power and authority of those who make decisions and ascertaining to whom they may render account. So far, the literature has mainly been concerned with how decisions are made, with a view to assessing to what extent a more efficient and coherent foreign and security policy is developing. In this contribution, institutions and decision-making procedures have been analysed through the lens of democracy rather than efficiency.

It follows from the above that the empirical aim has been modest. The conclusions should be read as a first stab at producing a more stringent analysis of the nature and form of integration in the field of foreign and security policy. I have sought to establish an analytical scheme that makes it possible to identify a move beyond intergovernmentalism as well as its putative democratic implications. Further, I have provided some examples of what it would take to corroborate such a thesis.

The analysis conducted here also casts the net wider than most studies of democracy in CFSP. Claims of a democratic deficit are usually derived from analyses of the (limited) powers of the EP. But what if the CFSP is intergovernmental? So far, the literature on the EP and the EU's foreign and security policy has touched too lightly on the fact that the EP's claims for more powers are difficult to justify within an intergovernmental system. A democratic cure is often proposed without a particularly thorough discussion of the diagnosis. The analysis here contributes to the latter.

Given that foreign and security policy is only to a limited extent subject to democratic scrutiny at the national level, the conclusions presented are perhaps no surprise. However, what is surprising is that member states have voluntarily surrendered power to a larger entity. This challenges existing assumptions about foreign and security policy, as well as conventional wisdom regarding foreign policy as the ultimate guardian of sovereignty.

The CFSP does not simply perpetuate the traditions established at the national level through intergovernmental arrangements. It contributes to remove foreign and security policy further from citizens' influence. Executive dominance in this field has been reinforced to the detriment of the legislative branch; yet equally striking is the fragmentation of the (executive) foreign-policy apparatus. National foreign and security policies are integrated in a semi-autonomous institutional structure, which has developed a 'higher order' conception of *European* interests and values.

Further research is required in order to account for this voluntary surrendering of power and authority to a larger entity. This is a real puzzle to conventional international relations theory. Also, if the CFSP is no longer intergovernmental, then what is it, and how can it be democratic? In this contribution I have not addressed the question of what might constitute adequate institutional solutions to the democratic challenges of the CFSP. However, findings here suggest that these challenges are of a slightly different character from the core of the EU, owing to the diffuse status of CFSP as neither intergovernmental nor supranational.

Biographical note: Helene Sjursen is Professor at ARENA – Centre for European Studies, University of Oslo, Norway.

ACKNOWLEDGEMENTS

Many thanks to Erik O. Eriksen and Ian Cooper, as well to two anonymous referees, for detailed and helpful comments on this contribution. Research conducted for this paper was supported by a grant from the Norwegian Ministry of

Defence. The paper is a contribution to the RECON project, financed by the 6th Framework Programme of the European Commission.

NOTE

1 'External Action of the EU: General Debate', Comment number 4-031, p. 16. Minutes of the Convention meeting of 11 July 2002. Available at http://www.diss. fu-berlin.de/diss/servlets/MCRFileNodeServlet/FUDISS_derivate_000000005252/ Hatakoy_Dissertation_4.pdf;jsessionid=A2C0C11FB5631D87C9D8EE7843565F 84hosts= (accessed 21 September 2011).

REFERENCES

Aggestam, L. (2004) *A European Foreign Policy? Role Conceptions and the Politics of Identity in Britain, France and Germany*, Stockholm University: Department of Political Science.

Allen, D. (1998) 'Who speaks for Europe? The search for an effective and coherent external policy', in J. Peterson and H. Sjursen (eds), *A Common Foreign Policy for Europe?* London: Routledge, pp. 41–58.

Arrow, K.J. (1985) 'The economics of agency', in J.W. Pratt and R.J. Zeckhauser (eds), *Principals and Agents: The Structure of Business*, Cambridge, MA: Harvard Business School Press, pp. 37–51.

Barbé, E. (2004) 'The evolution of CFSP institutions: where does democratic accountability stand?', *The International Spectator* 39(2): 47–60.

Bono, G. (2006) 'Challenges of democratic oversight of EU security policies', *European Security* 15(4): 431–49.

Bovens, M., Curtin, D. and Hart, P. (eds) (2010) *The Real World of EU Accountability: What deficit?* Oxford: Oxford University Press.

Cremona, M. (2008) 'Coherence through law: what difference will the Treaty of Lisbon make?', *Hamburg Review of Social Sciences* 3(1): 11–36.

Crum, B. (2009) 'Accountability and personalisation of the European Council Presidency', *European Integration* 31(6): 685–701.

Council of the European Union (2003) 'A secure Europe in a better world: European Security Strategy', Brussels, 12 December.

Council of the European Union (2008) 'Report on the implementation of the European Security Strategy – providing security in a changing world', *S407/08*, Brussels, 11 December.

Dahl, R.A. (1989) *Democracy and its Critics*, New Haven, CT: Yale University Press.

Diedrichs, U. (2004) 'The European Parliament in CFSP: more than a marginal player?', *The International Spectator* 39(2): 31–46.

Duke, S. (2004) 'The linchpin COPS: assessing the workings and institutional relations of the Political and Security Committee', *European Institute of Public Administration Working Paper 05/5*, Maastricht: EIPA.

Duke, S. and Vanhoonacker, S. (2006) 'Administrative governance and CFSP', in H.C.H. Hofmann and A.H. Türk (eds), *EU Administrative Governance*, Cheltenham: Edward Elgar, pp. 361–87.

Eriksen, E.O. (2009) *The Unfinished Democratization of Europe*, Oxford: Oxford University Press.

Eriksen, E.O. and Fossum, J.E. (2011) 'Bringing European democracy back in: or how to read the German Constitutional Court's Lisbon Treaty ruling', *European Law Journal* 17(2): 153–71.

European Parliament (2010) 'Debate on the European External Action Service, European Parliament', *CRE 07/07/2010-12*, European Parliament, Strasbourg, 7 July, available at http://www.europarl.europa.eu/sides/getDoc.do?pubRef=-//EP//TEXT+CRE+20100707?+ITEM-012+DOC+XML+V0//EN (accessed 21 September 2011).

Frankenberg, G. (2000) 'The return of the contract: problems and pitfalls of European constitutionalism', *European Law Journal* 6(3): 257–76.

Habermas, J. (1996) *Between Facts and Norms*, Cambridge, MA: MIT Press.

Held, D. (2006) *Models of Democracy*, 3rd edn, Cambridge: Polity Press.

Hill, C. (1993) 'Shaping a federal foreign policy for Europe', in B. Hocking (ed.), *Managing Foreign Relations in Federal States*, London: Leicester University Press, pp. 268–83.

House of Commons (2008) 'Foreign policy aspects of the Lisbon Treaty', *Third Report of Session 2007-08, HC-120I*, London, 20 January.

Howorth, J. (2001) 'European defence and the changing politics of the European Union: hanging together or hanging separately?', *Journal of Common Market Studies* 39(4): 765–89.

Howorth, J. (2010) 'The Political and Security Committee: a case study in "supranational inter-governmentalism"', *Les Cahiers europeens de Sciences Po, No. 01/2010*, available at http://www.cee.sciences-po.fr/erpa/docs/wp_2010_1.pdf

Joachim, J. and Dembinski, M. (2011) 'A contradiction in terms? NGOs, democracy, and European Foreign and Security Policy', *Journal of European Public Policy* 18(8): 1151–68.

Juncos, A.E. and Pomorska, K. (2006) 'Playing the Brussels game: strategic socialisation in the CFSP Council Working Groups', *European Integration on-line Papers (EIoP)* 10(11).

Juncos, A.E. and Pomorska, K. (2011) 'Invisible and unaccountable? National representatives and council officials in EU foreign policy', *Journal of European Public Policy* 18(8): 1096–1114.

Juncos, A.E. and Reynolds, C. (2007) 'The Political and Security Committee: governing in the shadow', *European Foreign Affairs Review* 12: 127–47.

Jørgensen, K.E. (ed.) (2009) *The European Union and International Organisations*, London: Routledge.

Keohane, R., Macedo, S. and Moravcsik, A. (2009) 'Democracy-enhancing multilateralism', *International Organization* 63: 1–31.

Lord, C. (2011a) 'Polecats, lions, and foxes: coasian bargaining theory and attempts to legitimate the Union as a constrained form of political power', *European Political Science Review* 3(1): 83–102.

Lord, C. (2011b) 'The political theory and practice of Parliamentary participation in the Common Security and Defence Policy', *Journal of European Public Policy* 18(8): 1133–50.

Majone, G. (2001) 'Two logics of delegation: agency and fiduciary relations in EU governance', *Euroepan Union Politics* 2(1): 103–21.

Maurer, A., Kietz, D. and Völkel, C. (2005) 'Interinstitutional agreements in the CFSP: Parliamentarization through the back door?', *European Foreign Affairs Review* 10: 175–95.

Meyer, C. (2006) *The Quest for a European Strategic Culture: Changing Norms on Security and Defence in the European Union*, Basingstoke: Palgrave Macmillan.

Moravcsik, A. (1998) *The Choice for Europe: Social Purpose and State Power from Messina to Maastricht*, London: University College London Press.

Nuttall, S. (2000) *European Foreign Policy*, Oxford: Oxford University Press.

Peters, D., Wagner, W. and Deitelhoff, N. (2008) 'Parliaments and security policy: mapping the Parliamentary field', in D. Peters, W. Wagner and N. Deitelhoff (eds), *The Parliamentary Control of European Security Policy*, ARENA Report 7/ 2008, Oslo: ARENA Centre for European Studies, pp. 3–28.

Pettit, P. (1997) *Republicanism: A Theory of Freedom and Government*, Oxford: Oxford University Press.

Pijpers, A. (1996) 'The Netherlands: the weakening pull of Atlanticism', in C. Hill (ed.), *The Actors in Europe's Foreign Policy*, London: Routledge, pp. 247–67.

Pollack, M.A. (2003) *The Engines of European Integration: Delegation, Agency and Agenda Setting in the EU*, Oxford: Oxford University Press.

Puetter, U. (2003) 'Informal circles of ministers: a way out of the EU's institutional dilemmas?', *European Law Journal* 9(1): 109–24.

Rawls, J. (1993) *Political Liberalism*, New York: Columbia University Press.

Riddervold, M. and Sjursen, H. (forthcoming, 2012) 'Playing into the hands of the Commission? Accounting for the impact of international organisations on EU foreign policy', in O. Costa and K.E. Jørgensen (eds), *The Influence of International Institutions on the EU: When Multilateralism Hits Brussels*, Basingstoke: Palgrave.

Sjursen, H. (2003) 'Understanding the Common Foreign and Security Policy: analytical building blocs', in M. Knodt and S. Princen (eds), *Understanding the European Union's External Relations*, London: Routledge, pp. 35–53.

Smith, M.E. (2001) 'The quest for coherence: institutional dilemmas of external action from Maastricht to Amsterdam', in A. Stone Sweet, W. Sanholtz and N. Fligstein (eds), *The Institutionalisation of Europe*, Oxford: Oxford University Press, pp. 170–93.

Smith, M.E. (2004) *Europe's Foreign and Security Policy: The Institutionalization of Cooperation*, Cambridge: Cambridge University Press.

Thym, D. (2006) 'Beyond Parliament's reach? The role of the European Parliament in the CFSP', *European Foreign Affairs Review* 11: 109–27.

Thym, D. (2011) 'The Intergovernmental branch of the EU's Foreign Affairs Executive: reflections on the Political and Security Committee', in H.-J. Blanke and S. Mangiameli (eds), *The European Union after Lisbon: Constitutional Basis, Economic Order and External Action*, Heidelberg: Springer, pp. 517–532.

Tonra, B. (2000) 'Committees in common: committee governance and CFSP', in T. Christiansen and E. Kirchner (eds), *Committee Governance in the European Union*, Manchester: Manchester University Press, pp. 145–60.

Tonra, B. (2003) 'Constructing the Common Foreign and Security Policy: the utility of a cognitive approach', *Journal of Common Market Studies* 42(4): 731–56.

Torreblanca, J. (2001) 'Ideas, preferences and institutions', *ARENA Working Paper 26/ 2001*, Oslo: ARENA.

Vanhoonacker, S., Dijsktra, H. and Maurer, H. (2010) Understanding the role of bureaucracy in the European Security and Defence Policy: the state of the art, in Vanhoonacker, S., Dijkstra, H. amd Maurer, H. (2010), *Understanding the Role of Bureaucracy in the European Security and Defence Policy, European integration online Papers (EIoP)*, Special Issue 1(14), available at http://eiop.or.at/eiop/texte/ 2010-004a.htm (accessed 21 September 2011).

Invisible and unaccountable? National Representatives and Council Officials in EU foreign policy

Ana E. Juncos and Karolina Pomorska

ABSTRACT The role of officials from the working groups and the Council Secretariat dealing with European Union (EU) external relations has grown in recent years as a result of the increase in the thematic and geographic scope of EU foreign policy and, in particular, the development of the EU's capabilities in crisis management. The increase in competences of Brussels-based bodies has occurred in parallel to a transformation of the policy-making process that challenges intergovernmentalist assumptions about the extent of the control exercised by the member states over foreign policy-making. This contribution tracks the impact of Brusselization and socialization processes on Council officials and national representatives, which has resulted in these actors playing a role beyond that foreseen in the original delegation mandate. This inevitably raises questions of accountability in EU foreign policy.

INTRODUCTION

Despite countless Treaty reforms, the Common Foreign and Security Policy (CFSP) remains obstinately intergovernmental, or so it may be assumed from the provisions contained in the Lisbon Treaty. National representatives working in this policy area are expected to remain under strict instructions from, and accountable to, the member states, whereas Council officials are required to perform their task of assisting the Council and its Presidency in a professional and neutral manner. However, informal developments have led to some commentators pointing to the gradual erosion of lines of accountability in this policy area. Above all, the potential impact of socialization among Council officials – what some have referred to as 'going native' – would imply a departure from a purely intergovernmental decision-making. From an accountability perspective, this is particularly problematic given the increasing executive and quasi-legislative role of Council working groups and the Council Secretariat General in European Union (EU) foreign policy (Curtin and Egeberg 2008). Therefore, it is important to ascertain whether officials working in the Council either remain faithful representatives of their country and act upon the call of their principals at home — in the case of the Council working groups — or perform a neutral secretarial role as envisaged by the Treaties — in the case of the Council Secretariat.

This contribution aims at providing an empirical examination of some claims made in the literature about the significance of Brusselization and socialization processes for the democratic deficit of European foreign policy by looking at the cases of the Council working groups and the Secretariat General. Despite the increasing empirical attention paid to the CFSP institutional machinery, these two case studies remain under-researched in the literature. The underlying assumption is that without knowing what happens behind the closed doors of the Council, or as Helene Sjursen (2007: 2) put it, without studying 'the complex institutional "soup" of the CFSP', it is difficult to make any specific claims about the existence of a democratic deficit. Nevertheless, the aim of this contribution is not to provide a full discussion of accountability, but to provide the empirical backdrop for wider discussions raised by others in this collection.

Thus, the aim of this paper is threefold. First, it will uncover the ongoing processes of Brusselization and socialization that have taken place in the CFSP. It pays special attention to processes of informal institutionalization at the committee level and in the Council Secretariat. This analysis will allow us to determine the role of these two institutions in the policy-making process and whether national representatives and Council officials have acquired additional tasks that were not foreseen when their institutions were originally designed. Second, this contribution seeks to determine the impact of socialization on the individuals involved in the decision-making process. It aims to better understand how socialization affects co-operation patterns and national positions in the case of the Council working group members; and their roles and loyalties in the case of Council Secretariat officials. Third, it seeks to establish the challenges this might raise from an accountability perspective and whether the changes introduced by the Lisbon Treaty might address these challenges and/or raise new ones. With the entry into force of the Lisbon Treaty (1 December 2009), the role of the working groups remains a vital one in the overall decision-making process, although an important aspect has changed: most of the CFSP working groups are now chaired by a representative of the High Representative. The role of the Council Secretariat has been more critically affected, since many of its officials have been relocated to the newly created European External Action Service (EEAS). Although the empirical evidence presented in this contribution only covers the period up to 2010, it is argued that many of the accountability challenges identified in the pre-Lisbon period still remain problematic after the entry into force of the Treaty.

Before turning to these issues, a brief methodological note is in order. This contribution is based on fieldwork conducted by both authors in Brussels between 2004 and 2010. The data was collected through 50 interviews with national representatives and 46 interviews with Council Secretariat officials.

In addition, 45 questionnaires were filled in by officials from the Council Secretariat General and by 28 national representatives to the Council working groups. In September and November 2010 interviews were also conducted with officials from the European Commission, Directorate-General for External Relations (DG Relex).

BEYOND INTERGOVERNMENTALISM?

While the reforms introduced at Amsterdam, Nice and Lisbon have changed the institutional configuration and policy scope of the CFSP, formally this policy has remained intergovernmental as far as the policy-making process is concerned. Despite the abolition of pillars with the Lisbon Treaty, the CFSP 'is subject to specific rules and procedures' (Article 24, TEU Lisbon). Unanimity continues to be the rule, especially in the Common Security and Defence Policy (CSDP), qualified majority voting the exception. Two new Declarations also remind us that the Treaty shall not affect the member states' ability to formulate and implement their foreign policy (Declaration 13, Lisbon Treaty) and that provisions in the Treaty do not give new powers to the Commission or the European Parliament (Declaration 14, Lisbon Treaty).

However, intergovernmentalism, understood as a decision-making process whereby 'member states continue to control decision-making' (Jorgensen, quoted in Øhrgaard 2004: 28; Sjursen 2011), and the characterization of CFSP as an 'intergovernmental' policy blatantly fail to account for 'the practices of European foreign policy co-operation which have emerged over the years, and the impact which they have had' (Øhrgaard 2004: 28). Scholars looking at the development of CFSP/CSDP have routinely noted that '[w]hile there is therefore no "communitarization" of CFSP decision-making, a system is under construction that has certainly moved away from formal intergovernmentalism' (Tonra 2003: 733; Howorth 2001; Sjursen 2007). Two interlinked processes seem to have contributed to this erosion of pure intergovernmentalism: Brusselization and socialization. Brusselization, meaning the gradual shift of foreign-policy authority from the capitals to Brussels (Allen 1998: 54) is said to have been taking place since the establishment of the CFSP and it continues to this day. The Lisbon Treaty has furthered Brusselization by strengthening the role of the High Representative and by creating the new EEAS, including officials from the European Commission, the Council Secretariat General and the member states. Because of the growing institutional complexity, the intensity of negotiations, and the distance from the locus of decision-making, Brusselization weakens the control exercised by the member states on the decision-making process.

Socialization raises even more challenges. We understand socialization broadly as a process by which social interaction leads novices to endorse group norms (Johnston 2001: 493), which may result in the establishment of a 'we-feeling' among the policy-makers and, in time, lead to emergence of a common 'role identity'. In this contribution, we focus on the emerging new norms and 'we-feeling' in the case of the working groups and on the acquisition of new roles in the case of the Council Secretariat. Norms in this context can be defined as the '(unwritten) rules that prescribe the attitudes and behaviours that are (or are not) appropriate in the context of the group' (Nijstad and van Knippenberg 2008: 250). These norms can be either substantive (e.g., democracy, rule of law or free trade) or behavioural (e.g., neutrality, consensus-building or co-ordination reflex). The latter are particularly relevant in the case of Council working groups and officials as discussed below. Roles are based upon the expectations that are held by actors regarding their own behaviour or the behaviour of others (Biddle 1986: 67). These roles are closely linked to institutional norms, since they comprise a set of norms that should or should not be applicable in certain situations. Socialization would therefore lead group-members to a consistent compliance with the group's norms regardless of whether they have been internalized or not. This is ensured through social sanctioning, i.e., those individuals who adhere to the in-group norms are approved of, while those who do not comply with the norms are disapproved of, or even punished (Turner 1991: 3).

From an intergovernmental perspective, EU member states delegate tasks to their representatives in the working groups to facilitate co-operation with other member states and to reduce transaction costs. In the same vein, the Council of the European Union delegates some powers or tasks to its General Secretariat in order to ensure the overall effectiveness of the decision-making process (Dijkstra 2010). From the perspective of a principal–agent framework, agency loss might occur because rational agents deviate from their delegation mandate so as to maximize their preferences (Pollack 1997; Tallberg 2002). Challenging the intergovernmental take on relations between principals and agents, the underlying assumption of this study is that socialization of national representatives and Council officials may lead to changes in their behaviour, and even preferences, which in turn may result in a loss in control by the capitals/Council. This happens in the case of the working groups when the representatives do not fully respect their mandates or try to influence/shape them because of the need to comply with group norms; and in the case of the Council Secretariat when actors get socialized into new roles which are not officially delegated to them. In this way, socialization among national representatives and officials in the Council transforms the policy-making process beyond intergovernmentalism, which in turn has important implications in terms of accountability.

Socialization transforms the policy-making processes in Brussels as some norms become a part of an informal 'code of conduct' in the Council committees. These unwritten rules are generally acknowledged and observed by the group members. Even if one considers this process in rationalist terms – i.e., actors follow the rules as part of a rational calculus to maintain their credibility, improve their reputation or because of material gains – it might lead to actors introducing changes to their original instructions in the case of Council working group officials; or – in the case of Council Secretariat officials – to actors adopting new political and executive functions beyond the administrative and supportive tasks with which they had been entrusted. If and when internalization occurs, socialization will result in even more challenges to delegation as it might lead to changes in preferences and a shift of loyalties and identities.

While Brusselization and socialization are inextricably linked, these two concepts are not interchangeable. Brusselization refers to a physical move of the CFSP governance system (and those officials involved) to Brussels; socialization, on the other hand, is a behavioural and cognitive process involving changes in behaviour, attitudes and/or beliefs. The concept of Brusselization refers to a process of institutionalization, understood as the creation or development of formal and informal institutions, with a particular locus in Brussels. Brusselization is hence a necessary condition to spark socialization: by bringing diplomats and officials into frequent, intense and insulated interactions (Tonra 2000: 158), Brussels-based institutions have facilitated socialization processes.

The paper first examines processes of Brusselization over time, before proceeding to analyse the potential impact of socialization on the diplomats and officials working in the Council working groups and the Council Secretariat. Finally, conclusions are drawn with respect to the potential implications this study has for the implementation of the Lisbon Treaty and the emerging EEAS.

A BRUSSELIZED EU FOREIGN POLICY

Over the lifetime of the European Political Co-operation (EPC) and the CFSP, we have witnessed a remarkable process of institutionalization with an increasing number of policy-making capabilities shifted to Brussels. The case of Council working groups and the Council Secretariat best epitomize this 'Brusselization' process. With the establishment of the EPC, a number of working groups were created to support the work of European Communities (EC) foreign ministers. However, until the signing of the Single European Act (SEA), these working groups met in the capital of the member state holding the Presidency, alongside the meetings of the political directors and the foreign ministers. With the establishment of a single institutional framework and the CFSP in the Treaty of Maastricht (1991), the EPC working groups were merged with their communitarian counterparts, the EC working parties.

Gradually, the merger has led to the Brusselization of the CFSP decision-making process, with a progressive move of national representatives to Brussels. Representatives in the CFSP working groups are increasingly diplomats based at the Permanent Representations in Brussels, whereas the number of 'capital formations' meetings[1] has decreased to an average of twice per Presidency. In addition, the change has not only affected the composition, but also the role of the working groups, which have become much more 'legislative' and bureaucratic in nature, drafting Council acts and focusing on operational issues. There are currently 36 permanent working groups dealing with foreign affairs, organized along thematic and geographical lines (see Council of the European Union 2010a).

The SEA also created a permanent EPC Secretariat. Until then, the EPC had not had a permanent secretariat, as some member states feared a loss of sovereignty in the foreign policy field. Instead, the rotating Presidency was responsible for providing administrative support. The new Secretariat introduced by the SEA was based upon 'an extended troika', staffed with 17 officials, mostly from the previous, current and following Presidency, plus an archivist, administrative and communication staff and a Head of Secretariat (Tonra 2000: 153). With the Maastricht Treaty, the EPC Secretariat merged with the Council Secretariat, consolidating the Brusselization of this bureaucracy. While the Secretariat has undergone a profound transformation in recent years, the creation of the post of the High Representative in the Amsterdam Treaty (1999), supported by an Early Warning and Policy Unit (hereafter Policy Unit), further transformed the nature of the Council Secretariat, adding a political function to its traditional administrative one. Yet, the most important development in the last few years was the extension of the Council Secretariat's responsibility in CSDP to carry out planning and executive functions. New units were created in DG-E (External and Political-Military Affairs) to manage civilian crisis management operations and the political-military aspects of CSDP. The creation of the EU Military Staff (EUMS) in 2001 and the establishment of the Civilian Planning and Conduct Capability (CPCC) and the Crisis Management and Planning Directorate (CMPD) also increased the planning and operational capacities of the Council Secretariat in the field of military and civilian crisis management. At the time of writing, a new restructuration is ongoing as a result of the implementation of the Lisbon Treaty.

An increasing role in the policy-making process

The creation and relocation of foreign-policy bodies to Brussels has taken place alongside an increase in the competences and influence of these bodies in the policy-making process. Similar developments have been noted in other policy areas with Carol Harlow (2002: 34) arguing that 'decisions have in effect – though not of course legally – been passed to a corps of invisible and unaccountable public servants'. Given the sensitivities in the foreign policy area, it is crucial to determine whether this is actually the case.

Turning our attention first to the Council working groups, it is necessary to determine how much is decided in the working groups, before the dossier goes to higher levels, such as the Committee of Permanent Representatives (COREPER) and the Foreign Affairs Council (FAC). Traditionally, the assumption has been that the foreign ministers hold tight control over issues discussed in Brussels. However, the first studies of the Council working groups' role in decision-making pointed to a surprisingly high percentage of decisions already agreed at the lower level. In a well-known study of the Council, Fiona Hayes-Renshaw and Helen Wallace (1997: 40, 78) estimated that approximately 70 per cent of the total number of items on the General Affairs and External Relations Council (GAERC) agenda had been previously agreed in the working groups and 15–20 per cent in COREPER. These estimates were widely cited by researchers looking at the role of working groups and committees (Beyers and Dierickx 1998: 291; Lewis 1998: 483), including in foreign and security policies (Duke and Vanhoonacker 2006: 169; Juncos and Pomorska 2006: 5).

More recent studies on Council decision-making have challenged these figures. Drawing on cross-sectoral data about involvement of different levels in the decision-making, Frank M. Häge (2008) argues that almost 50 per cent of all decisions in the Community pillar are discussed by the ministers, and almost one-third of them are decided at this level. In the area of external relations, however, his findings point at a much lower degree of involvement by ministers: only 1 out of 17 decisions (approximately 6 per cent) was decided by GAERC. This can be explained by the fact that Häge's data only examines legislative acts with the involvement of the European Parliament, which only represent a small percentage in foreign policy. Another study by Ricardo Gomez and John Peterson (2001) examined the ministerial agendas of the General Affairs Council (GAC) during the period 1995–2000 and concluded that more than 50 per cent of the items were actually discussed in GAC as B points, while only 48 per cent were adopted as A points. However, the problem with this study was that it preceded the launch of the CSDP. In the second edition of their work on the Council, Hayes-Renshaw and Wallace (2006) also provided higher estimates of the involvement of GAERC in decision-making and put it at 31 per cent.

Our calculations suggest that around 39 per cent of the points in the ministerial agenda were debated by the FAC as B points during the period from January to November 2010 (authors' own calculations; Council of the European Union 2010b). Thus, while there are still some variations between the data provided by different studies, it would seem safe to assume that around a third of the decisions are discussed in ministerial meetings. If we also assume that 15–20 per cent of the decisions are discussed in COREPER (Hayes-Renshaw and Wallace 1997; Häge 2008), this means that approximately 40–45 per cent of the decisions are agreed at the level of the Council working groups. While this is much lower than previous estimates, it does not alleviate concerns about accountability in this policy area, as a high percentage of decisions (around two-thirds) are still taken without the involvement of ministers. Having said that, more research needs to be done to ascertain what type of decisions (politically sensitive or technical) are agreed at lower levels and at what stage working groups get involved.

For its part, the Council Secretariat, was initially seen as merely 'serving note-taking and "paper pusher" functions, lowering the transaction costs for work no one else wanted to be responsible for' (Lewis 2006: 6). However, time has proven that the initial fears of the capitals were not without reason, as some authors have argued that the Council Secretariat has been developing in the direction of an executive office (Christiansen and Vanhoonacker 2008; Curtin and Egeberg 2008) or a 'quasi executive agency making policy on its own' (Christiansen 2006: 89) with an entrepreneurial role (Lewis 2006: 7; Dijkstra 2010; Juncos and Pomorska 2010) rather than as a traditional secretariat.

The move from merely administrative function to the more executive and political tasks has been confirmed by our study of the Council Secretariat's roles (Juncos and Pomorska 2010). We asked officials about the tasks they perform in their everyday work (Table 1). As we can see from the data, the traditional task of the Secretariat to provide administrative support to Council meetings came only in sixth place. The task considered to be most important was 'to provide with information and common analysis', followed by 'supporting the Presidency' and 'identifying new policy problems and devise new policies'. This highlights the high ambitions and the willingness to play an active role in the design of European foreign policy by Council Secretariat officials.

The increasing role of the Council working groups and the Council Secretariat in the decision-making process does not challenge a traditional intergovernmental approach to the CFSP, providing that the member states ultimately remain in control and ensure that officials stick to their original instructions. However, socialization processes challenge this assumption, as discussed below.

SOCIALIZATION IN EU FOREIGN POLICY: GOING NATIVE?

Council working groups

Socialization among national representatives to the Council working groups is facilitated by the increasing frequency, intensity and insularity of contacts within 'Brusselized' institutions. The specific nature of CFSP institutions corresponds to some of the scope conditions that have been identified in the literature on socialization (Hooghe 2001; Beyers 2005; Checkel 2005). As argued by Jeffrey Lewis, institutional settings that exhibit high interaction intensity and high levels of insulation will 'deepen the mutual trust and introspection needed to routinize more co-operative styles of negotiation' (Lewis 2010: 652); what is more, 'institutional environments can work to place limits on instrumentalism and soften the cognitive boundaries of how self interest is conceptualized' (Lewis 2010: 649).

As far as the frequency of contacts is concerned, most Council working groups dealing with foreign policy issues meet at least once a week; some of them twice a week for instance, those dealing with the Western Balkans and with Eastern Europe and Central Asia. On top of formal contacts, informal contacts among national representatives also take place on a weekly basis. As important as the frequency of interaction is the quality and intensity of interaction (ibid.: 655) which has to do with whether representatives are being shuttled from their national capitals or based in their Permanent Representations. In the case of the Council working groups, they are permanently based in Brussels as a norm. This has a clear impact on the atmosphere of the meetings which is much more friendly and consensus-driven than 'capital formation' meetings.[2]

According to Hayes-Renshaw and Wallace (quoted in Lewis 2010: 655), the high frequency of interaction 'encourages a dense form of collegiality and

Table 1 Individual tasks of officials in Council Secretariat ranked in order of priority

	Provide with information and common analysis	Support the Presidency	Identify new problems and policies	Provide expertise for CSDP operations	Mediate conflicts	Provide administrative support	Defend the Council Secretariat prerogatives	Promote specific national interests
Mean	6.31	5.82	4.44	3.29	3.11	2.89	1.64	0.16
N	45	45	45	45	45	45	45	45

Source: Authors' own data.
Note: Values represent mean of importance: 8 = most important; 1 = less important; 0 = N/A.

collective identity, such that a reference to "we" or "our" policy is as likely to be a collective EU position as to a national position'. The representatives remain in close contact through e-mails, telephone conversations and frequent meetings that occur in the corridors as well as over lunch. As a result, many issues that appear in the agenda are 'pre-cooked', especially the sensitive ones, and the formal meeting serves more as a 'theatre' where participants play their roles. As one representative claimed: 'there is plenty of information exchanged in between the formal meetings, to the extent that sometimes, you know how the meeting will go, who is going to say what, who is going to support what, especially in the important issues'.[3]

The frequent and intense contacts taking place within and outside committee meetings lead national representatives permanently based in Brussels to adopt a 'code of conduct' or 'rules of the game' (Juncos and Pomorska 2006). One of the key procedural norms that national diplomats adopt is the co-ordination reflex, or a process of consultation and information-sharing with the rest of member states before a decision has been taken (see also Smith 2004: 122). Our research on CFSP Council working groups showed that a majority of respondents (83.9 per cent) consulted other national delegations prior to formal meetings 'always' or 'most of the time'.[4] A high percentage of respondents (96.4 per cent) stated that they consult with other delegations at least once a month.[5] The exchange of information takes place through formal channels such as the COREU Terminal System or CORTESY network (see Bicchi 2011) and official mailing lists. Nonetheless, a large bulk of information-sharing is informal.

Another norm identified is the consensus-building practice when it comes to the adoption of decisions, by contrast to hard-bargaining or confrontational methods (Smith 2004). Summarizing the significance of this practice, a national representative stated: 'in CFSP you can always say no. And if you are really serious about your no, nobody can stop you from blocking it. But this is rarely seen'.[6] According to our survey among representatives to the Council Working Groups, 96.4 per cent of the respondents stated that consensus-building rather than hard-bargaining was the predominant behaviour in CFSP negotiations.[7] Research on COREPER (Lewis 2005), Political and Security Committee (PSC) (Meyer 2006; Juncos and Reynolds 2007; Howorth 2010) and other CSDP committees (Cross 2010) confirms these findings. Member states' diplomats try to generate a broad agreement regarding the decision, to avoid the isolation of any member state in the decision-making process.

In the Council system, much of the consensus-seeking and co-operative culture stems from the set-up of negotiations. As well as the frequency and intensity of negotiations discussed above, insulation also plays a role. As has been noted in the literature, co-operative decision-making is facilitated by 'in camera' settings (Puetter 2003) such as the one we observe in the Council working groups. As mentioned elsewhere, CFSP can only work in a confidential environment (Hyde-Price 2003: 55). Meetings in the working groups take place behind closed doors and only representatives from the national delegations, the Commission and the Council Secretariat can attend. According to Jeffrey Lewis, such 'in-camera settings help facilitate co-operative styles of negotiation because they enable speaking frankly, explaining problems and expecting mutual responsiveness under a long shadow of the future' (Lewis 2010: 652). Secrecy thus has the 'collective effect of disciplining the pursuit of national interests' (ibid.) as representatives will need to justify their national positions or their decision to veto within the group.

Insulation not only refers to formal meetings, but also to informal ones (see Puetter 2003) whose frequency has increased after the 2004 and 2007 enlargements. In a context in which formal face-to-face contacts are increasingly difficult, enlargement has led to the creation of more informal negotiating forums and more informal contacts outside formal meetings. While secrecy and an increasing number of informal meetings are seen as a way in which to preserve the consensual atmosphere, they raise important questions in terms of transparency. Thus, a trade-off exists between striving for consensual decision-making and transparency. The institutionalization of like-minded groups can also be seen as a challenge to democratic practice because of the restricted and unequal access of its membership (Juncos and Pomorska 2008).

As well as a consensus-building norm, there is also a strong drive both among individual representatives and the member states to make the CFSP 'work'.[8] Part of this efficiency attitude is the determination to minimize the number of issues that are passed on to the higher level (COREPER or PSC). Hence, this also explains the high degree of involvement of working groups in the decision-making process as discussed above.

The commitment to make the CFSP 'work' also runs parallel to an increasing 'esprit de corps' among members of the group and the existence of a 'club-like atmosphere' (von der Gablentz 1979; Nuttall 1992). According to our survey, when national diplomats were asked about 'the degree of allegiance they feel to', the average rank was of 3.6 to their own national governments, 2.8 to the European Union and 2.4 to the CFSP working group in which they participate (1 = to a less extent; 4 = to a great extent). Although this data shows that national representatives still feel a strong loyalty to the national level in comparison to the EU or CFSP institutions, it also shows that this does not exclude a sense of loyalty towards the EU and their working group. Hence, this provides evidence of the 'Janus-like nature' of national diplomats in the Council working groups (Lewis 2005).

However, even if national representatives do not go native so easily, socialization processes do have an impact on their behaviour as they seek to comply with the in-group norms of co-ordination reflex and consensus-building. First, the co-ordination reflex, which predisposes national diplomats to take others' views into account, challenges the idea that national positions remain fixed (Juncos and Reynolds 2007: 144–6). Negotiations in Brussels have an impact on national positions as representatives sound out other delegations' positions and gather new information during meetings. Reports from the Council working groups meetings also play an important early warning role regarding possible conflicts with other member state positions. This might change initial positions and/or lead to the emergence of new preferences. It also helps develop a common under-standing among national representatives and fosters consensus-building.

The search for consensus and a desire to maintain the group's 'effectiveness' also challenges national positions and raises issues in terms of accountability. During interviews, diplomats emphasized that their capitals lack an overall sense of the atmosphere in the Council working groups and any experience concerning which positions have a chance of getting accepted and which arguments to use in order to convince other member states. Several national representatives empha-sized that there was nothing worse than receiving 'stupid' instructions with 'crazy ideas', which send them 'to die' or 'kill themselves' 'with an instruction which is completely out of the point'.[9] In order to avoid such situations, national represen-tatives seek to influence the instructions they receive from the capitals even before they are written. There are different ways of influencing the actual substance of instructions. These depend on the domestic organizational structure and the strength of the representative's own position within it. Some diplomats admit that on some occasions they are not given any precise instructions. For instance, a diplomat stated that 'what I do is write instructions for myself. I write [to my capital] what I am going to do, what I am going to say and unless I get something different, I proceed with this line'.[10] Others claim they act early to prevent receiving 'bad' instructions. There are also possibilities of negotiating changes during the Council meetings. Thus, it is a common practice that representatives either take phone calls quietly during negotiations or leave the room for a few minutes to discuss their positions with their capitals.

Council Secretariat General

As discussed earlier, in the pre-Lisbon period, new roles had been developed by the Council Secretariat in addition to its traditional administrative one. The Sec-retariat played an increasing role as a facilitator, providing information and common analysis and building consensus among member states; as a policy entrepreneur, identifying new policy problems and devising new policies; and as an implementation agent, providing expertise for the design and implemen-tation of CSDP operations. There was agreement among the interviewees that the role of the Secretariat should not be restricted to the administrative manage-ment of the Council meetings – 97 per cent of respondents 'strongly agreed' or 'agreed' with this view.[11] During the interviews, several officials emphasized the 'subtle' role of the Secretariat and that, despite the fact that credit always went to the Presidency, the Secretariat was in fact acting 'behind the scenes'.[12] One offi-cial claimed that the role of this institution was 'to influence the agenda-setting, developing content of the foreign policy and facilitating [negotiations] between the member states'.[13] This suggests that, prior to the implementation of the Lisbon Treaty, its role went beyond the traditional, administrative functions and thus challenged strictly intergovernmental understandings of European foreign policy by showing that socialization may lead to some unintended con-sequences in terms of delegation.

As mentioned above, the member states were, from the outset, very cautious about the creation of a permanent Secretariat in Brussels.[14] But when this happened, they made sure their officials were seconded to important positions in the Policy Unit of the High Representative or the EUMS. However, this did not alleviate fears, as it soon became obvious that national seconded officials ran the risk of 'going native' once exposed to the supranational institutional environment in Brussels, resulting in changes in their loyalties and a lack of sufficient control by the capitals. Our data shows that national seconded officials did not see themselves as 'national champions' in Brussels. On the contrary, a majority of nationally seconded officials (over 90 per cent) agreed that Council Secretariat officials should not take instructions from the member states – although, according to our survey, 65 per cent of respondents still admitted that there were instances when this occurred. Moreover, in line with the findings discussed earlier, a majority of nationally seconded officials (80 per cent) rejected the claim that the Secretariat's role should be restricted to the administrative management of dossiers and 60 per cent agreed that the Secretariat did have an impact on the substance of EU foreign policy.[15]

However, not everyone we spoke to agreed that these developments were a 'good thing'. This is indicative of normative tensions among the Secretariat staff (Juncos and Pomorska 2010). One official stated that the Secretariat should not even play a role of consensus facilitator between the member states, saying: 'I don't think it is expected of us to play such role, sometimes member states are better off without third party involvement – we should not take the initiative without the Presidency's indication.'[16] Another official noted that the Secretariat was a 'tool of the member states', a claim supported by other officials who described taking the initiative without the Presidency's involvement as 'inappropriate'.[17] Most of these criticisms of the Secretariat's entrepreneurial role came from *fonctionnaires* though, while nationally seconded officials seemed to be more comfortable with this state of affairs, which also indicated different socialization paths among Council Secretariat officials.

Council Secretariat officials were also keen to admit the independent impact that the Council Secretariat had on the CFSP/CSDP. A majority (97 per cent) agreed that the Council Secretariat should take an active part in designing EU foreign policy. In fact, two-thirds of officials admitted that the Council Secretariat did have an impact on the substance of the decisions. For instance, they argued that the Council Secretariat could 'contribute to define the [policy] line', use 'creative ways of moving things forward', 'influence the agenda-setting [process]' and 'develop the content of foreign policy'.[18] They also provided many examples of how they could influence the agenda-setting or content of some initiatives such as the status of forces agreement and the legal framework of the European Force (EUFOR) Atalanta mission.[19]

In relation to possible shifts in allegiances, a large majority of the interviewees saw themselves as 'very' or 'fairly' attached to both their countries and the European Union (see Figure 1). This shows that national and European identities co-exist. Interestingly, though, more officials saw themselves as 'very'

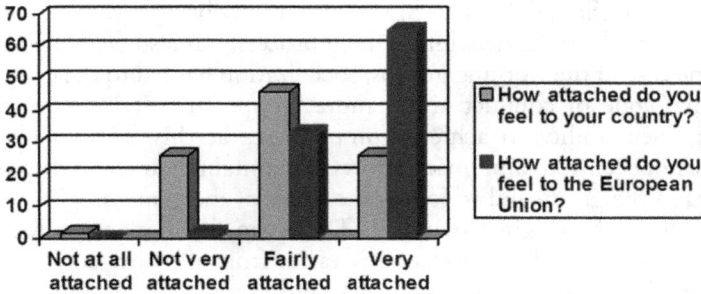

Figure 1 National and European identities among the officials of the Council Secretariat
Source: Authors' own data.
Note: Values (y-axis) represent percentage of the total.

attached to the European Union rather than to their countries. The shortcoming of this data, however, is that it only provides us with a snap-shot view and does not tell us by itself whether working in the Council Secretariat has caused any shift or whether it is just a matter of self-selection (i.e., those that have a stronger feeling of attachment to Europe decide to join EU institutions).

The increasing role of the Council Secretariat as a policy entrepreneur and its operation in the 'shadow of the Presidency' raises questions in terms of democratic accountability. Many of these developments, however, have been informal, hence remaining to a large extent unchallenged. The fact that the Council Secretariat is not subject to parliamentary oversight only increases concerns about any democratic deficit. Contacts between the Council Secretariat and the European Parliament are, in general, very limited. For instance, when asked about the external actors they met 'the most', none of the respondents from the Secretariat mentioned the European Parliament. A vast majority of officials also said they met officials from the European Parliament less than once a month.[20] This is not that worrying if we consider the Secretariat as a purely administrative body – after all, national administrators do not interact with the national parliaments either. However, if we consider the entrepreneurial and political roles developed by parts of the Secretariat such as the Policy Unit, then the non-existent contacts with the European Parliament do raise concerns. As most of these officials have now moved to the newly created EEAS, the question is whether more transparency and accountability can be better ensured.

CONCLUDING REMARKS

To date, diplomats from the Council working groups and officials from the Council Secretariat have remained largely invisible; however, given the increasing role of these actors in the decision-making process, their invisibility and lack of accountability raise legitimate concerns. This contribution argued that the

Brusselization of the CFSP and CSDP did not only bring officials together and increased their role in the decision-making process, but also facilitated socialization. In the case of the working groups, socialization has led to the emergence of an informal code of conduct and a more co-operative style of negotiations, increasing their ability to achieve compromises at this level. While loyalty shifts have not occurred, diplomats' efforts to maintain their credibility and reputation within the group and to follow the 'rules of the game' might still lead to deviations from the original mandate. The room for manoeuvre for national diplomats to re-write their instructions varies from member state to member state, depending on organizational issues, and requires a more in-depth study. In the case of the Council Secretariat, Brusselization and socialization resulted in the emergence of new, informal, more pro-active and entrepreneurial roles, not foreseen in the Treaties. The data also showed that the attachment of officials to the European Union was stronger than to their countries. Hence, the initial fears of the member states concerning the establishment of a permanent bureaucracy in Brussels were proven correct. Council Secretariat officials managed to have an impact on the agenda-setting and the policy substance which challenged an intergovernmental view of the CFSP.

Regarding secrecy as a challenge to accountability in European foreign policy, this contribution has shown that it is more of a problem in the case of the working groups, which have very restricted access and operate to a very large extent on an informal basis. The paradox between retaining an effective and consensual decision-making and achieving accountability continues to pose a challenge in this regard. In the case of the Council Secretariat, it was rather the fact that its impact in the decision-making process had been underestimated, despite the fact that officials had developed new entrepreneurial roles in addition to those envisaged in the treaties.

A few comments on the implications of Lisbon Treaty are in order. As for the working groups, the new High Representative for the Foreign Affairs and Security Policy (and officials acting on her behalf in the committees and working groups) has replaced the rotating Presidency in the CFSP area. This might reduce the opportunities for socialization that this position traditionally offered to the country at the helm. It was also seen as a significant 'restraining' mechanism as far as championing national interests was concerned. National representatives would act in a responsible and tempered way during their time holding the Presidency in the belief that other countries would act in a similar way. Yet, a permanent chair could facilitate consistency in the formulation of the agenda and could be seen as a more impartial mediator than the rotating Presidency. In any case, the Lisbon Treaty has not altered the Brusselization path and will not affect the intensity, frequency and insularity that have facilitated socialization thus far; if anything, it will intensify them.

Regarding the impact on the Council Secretariat, all officials dealing with foreign affairs are at the disposal of High Representative Ashton as a part of the EEAS. The new service consists of the permanent officials coming from the Commission and the Council Secretariat and the diplomats delegated from the member states. As far as the Council Secretariat is concerned, many of the officials with more proactive/political roles have been transferred to the EEAS. This may indicate the 'return' of the administrative Secretariat. However, with some of the working groups still being chaired by the rotating Presidency (in particular, those dealing with trade and development), there is still scope for an advisory and active role on the part of the Secretariat, especially in the case of inexperienced Presidencies and those from smaller member states.

The new institutional environment and organizational culture will influence the socialization processes of the EEAS officials. The current view in Brussels seems to be that the *esprit de corps* will take rather a long time to emerge given the amount of frustration and 'bad feelings' that exist today among delegated officials. Various interviewees suggested that team-building and training may be needed in order to foster this process.[21] It will be interesting to observe the impact that their experience in the EEAS might have on the nationally seconded officials and their behaviour after they return to their capitals. If the evidence from the Council Secretariat is anything to go by, nationally seconded officials, rather than acting as 'national champions', are likely to become socialized and adopt new roles that contribute to the strengthening of the new Brussels-based institutions.

Biographical notes: Ana E. Juncos is Lecturer in European Politics at the School of Sociology, Politics and International Studies, University of Bristol, United Kingdom. Karolina Pomorska is Assistant Professor at Maastricht University, The Netherlands.

ACKNOWLEDGEMENTS

The authors would like to thank the two anonymous referees and the participants at the ARENA Workshop 'Simply uploading executive power? Democracy and the Common Foreign and Security Policy of the European Union', Oslo, 7 October 2010, in particular Helene Sjursen and Deirdre Curtin. We are also grateful to Helen Drake, Alex Prichard, Paul Stephenson and Maarten Vink for their invaluable comments.

NOTES

1 This was the traditional composition of the EPC working groups, involving directors from the Ministries of Foreign Affairs, who would travel to the capital of the Presidency or to Brussels.

2 Interviews with national diplomats, Brussels, November 2005–January 2006.
3 *Ibid.*
4 Authors' own data, survey among national representatives to Council working groups, Brussels, October 2005–June 2006.
5 *Ibid.*
6 Interview with a national diplomat, Brussels, January 2006.
7 This view was echoed by Council Secretariat officials. Of the respondents to our survey, 80.4 per cent described the predominant mode in CFSP negotiations as one of consensus-building.
8 Interviews with national diplomats, Brussels, November 2005–January 2006.
9 *Ibid.*
10 Interview with a national diplomat, Brussels.
11 Authors' survey of Council Secretariat officials, Brussels, March–September 2009.
12 Interviews with Council Secretariat officials, 2009.
13 *Ibid.*
14 These fears of losing control over foreign affairs have not disappeared. They have been more than visible during the debate over the establishment of the EEAS (interviews with European Commission officials, September 2010).
15 Authors' survey of Council Secretariat officials, Brussels, March–September 2009.
16 Interview with a Council Secretariat official, Brussels, 2009.
17 *Ibid.*
18 *Ibid.*
19 *Ibid.*
20 Authors' survey of Council Secretariat officials, Brussels, March–September 2009.
21 Interviews with European Commission officials, Brussels, November 2010.

REFERENCES

Allen, D. (1998) 'Who speaks for Europe?,' in J. Peterson and H. Sjursen (eds), *A Common Foreign Policy for Europe? Competing Visions of CFSP*, London: Routledge, pp. 41–58.
Beyers, J. (2005) 'Multiple embeddedness and socialization in Europe: the case of Council Officials', *International Organization* 59: 899–936.
Beyers, J. and Dierickx, G. (1998) 'The working groups of the Council of the European Union: supranational or intergovernmental negotiations?', *Journal of Common Market Studies* 36(3): 289–317.
Bicchi, F. (2011) 'The EU as a community of practice: foreign-policy communications in the COREU network', *Journal of European Public Policy* 18(8): 1115–32.
Biddle, B.J. (1986) 'Recent developments in role theory', *Annual Review of Sociology* 12: 67–92.
Checkel, J. (2005) 'International organizations and socialization in Europe: introduction', *International Organization* 59(4): 801–26.
Christiansen, T. (2006) 'Out of shadows: the General Secretariat of the Council of Ministers', *The Journal of Legislative Studies* 8(4): 80–97.
Christiansen, T. and Vanhoonacker, S. (2008) 'At a critical juncture? Change and continuity in the institutional development of the Council Secretariat', *West European Politics* 31(4): 751–70.
Council of the European Union (2010a) , 'List of Council preparatory bodies', 12319/10, 20 July.
Council of the European Union (2010b) 'Agendas of meetings', available at http://www.consilium.europa.eu/showPage.aspx?id=643&lang=EN (accessed 3 December 2010).

Cross, M.K.D. (2010) 'Cooperation by committee: the EU Military Committee and the Committee for Civilian Crisis Management', *Occasional Paper 82*, Paris: EU Institute for Security Studies.

Curtin, D. and Egeberg, M. (2008) 'Tradition and innovation: Europe's accumulated executive order', *West European Politics* 31(4): 639–61.

Dijkstra, H. (2010) 'Explaining variation in the role of the EU Council Secretariat in the first and second pillar policy-making', *Journal of European Public Policy* 17(4): 527–44.

Duke, S. and Vanhoonacker, S. (2006) 'Administrative governance in CFSP: development and practice', *European Foreign Affairs Review* 11(2): 163–82.

Gomez, R. and Peterson, J. (2001) 'The EU's impossibly busy foreign ministers: "no one is in control"', *European Foreign Affairs Review* 6(1): 53–74.

Häge, F.M. (2008) 'Who decides in the Council of the European Union?', *Journal of Common Market Studies* 46(3): 533–58.

Harlow, C. (2002) *Accountability in the European Union*, Oxford: Oxford University Press.

Hayes-Renshaw, F. and Wallace, H. (1997) *The Council of Ministers*, Basingstoke: Macmillan.

Hayes-Renshaw, F. and Wallace, H. (2006) *The Council of Ministers*, 2nd edn, Basingstoke: Palgrave Macmillan.

Hooghe, L. (2001) *The European Commission and the Integration of Europe. Images of Governance*, Cambridge, MA: Cambridge University Press.

Howorth, J. (2001) 'European defence and the changing politics of the European Union: hanging together or hanging separately?', *Journal of Common Market Studies* 39(4): 765–89.

Howorth, J. (2010) 'The Political and Security Committee: a case study in "supranational intergovernmentalism"?' *Les Cahiers Européens 01/2010*, Centre d'Etudes Europeennes, Paris: SciencesPo.

Hyde-Price, A. (2003) 'Decision-making in the second pillar', in A. Arnull and D. Wincott (eds), *Accountability and Legitimacy in the European Union*, Oxford: Oxford University Press, pp. 41–62.

Johnston, A.I. (2001) 'Treating international institutions as social environments', *International Studies Quarterly* 45(4): 487–515.

Juncos, A.E. and Pomorska, K. (2006) 'Playing the Brussels game: strategic socialisation in the CFSP Council working groups', *European Integration online Papers (EIoP)* 10(11), available at http://eiop.or.at/eiop/index.php/eiop/article/view/2006_011a/34 (accessed 1 December 2010).

Juncos, A.E. and Pomorska, K. (2008) 'Does size matter? CFSP committees after enlargement', *Journal of European Integration* 30(4): 493–509.

Juncos, A.E. and Pomorska, K. (2010) , 'Secretariat, facilitator or policy entrepreneur? Role perceptions of officials of the Council Secretariat', in S. Vanhoonacker, H. Dijkstra and H. Maurer (eds), 'Understanding the role of bureaucracy in the European Security and Defence Policy', *European Integration online Papers (EIoP)*, special issue 1, vol. 14, available at http://www.eiop.or.at/eiop/index.php/eiop/article/viewFile/2010_007a/176 (accessed 1 December 2010).

Juncos, A.E. and Reynolds, C. (2007) 'The Political and Security Committee: governing in the shadow', *European Foreign Affairs Review* 12(2): 123–47.

Lewis, J. (1998) 'Is the "hard bargaining" image of the Council misleading? The Committee of Permanent Representatives and the Local Elections Directive', *Journal of Common Market Studies* 36(4): 479–504.

Lewis, J. (2005) 'The Janus face of Brussels: socialisation and everyday decision making in the European Union', *International Organization* 59(4): 937–71.

Lewis, J. (2006). 'Where informal rules rule: the Council General Secretariat and Presidency in everyday EU decision making', Paper presented at the *2006 International Studies Association Conference*, San Diego, 22–25 March.

Lewis, J. (2010) 'How institutional environments facilitate cooperative negotiation styles in the EU decision making', *Journal of European Public Policy* 17(5): 650–66.

Meyer, C.O. (2006) *The Quest for a European Strategic Culture. Changing Norms on Security and Defence in the European Union*, London: Palgrave Macmillan.

Nijstad, B.A. and van Knippenberg, D. (2008) 'The psychology of groups: basic principles', in M. Hewstone, W. Stroebe and K. Jonas (eds), *Introduction to Social Psychology. A European Perspective*, 4th edn, Oxford: Blackwell, pp. 244–62.

Nuttall, S.J. (1992) *European Political Co-Operation*, Oxford: Clarendon Press.

Pollack, M. (1997) 'Delegation, agency and agenda-setting in the European Community', *International Organization* 51(1): 99–134.

Puetter, U. (2003) 'Informal circles of ministers: a way out of the EU's institutional dilemmas?', *European Law Journal* 9(1): 109–24.

Sjursen, H. (2007) 'Integration without democracy? Three conceptions of European security policy in transformation', *RECON Online Working Paper 2007/19*, Oslo: ARENA.

Sjursen, H. (2011) 'The EU's Common Foreign and Security Policy: the quest for democracy', *Journal of European Public Policy* 18(8): 1069–77.

Smith, M.E. (2004) *Europe's Foreign and Security Policy. The Institutionalization of Cooperation*, Cambridge, MA: Cambridge University Press.

Tallberg, J. (2002) 'Delegation to supranational institutions: why, how and with what consequences?', *West European Politics* 25(1): 23–46.

Tonra, B. (2000) 'Committees in common: committee governance and CFSP', in T. Christiansen and E. Kirchner (eds), *Committee Governance in the European Union*, Manchester: Manchester University Press, pp. 145–60.

Tonra, B. (2003) 'Constructing the Common Foreign and Security Policy: the utility of a cognitive approach', *Journal of Common Market Studies* 41(4): 731–56.

Turner, C.T. (1991) *Social Influence*, Buckingham: Open University Press.

von der Gablentz, O. (1979) 'Luxembourg revisited or the importance of European political cooperation', *Common Market Law Review* 16: 685–99.

Øhrgaard, J.C. (2004) 'International relations or European integration: is the CFSP *sui generis?*,' in B. Tonra and T. Christiansen (eds), *Rethinking European Union Foreign Policy*, Manchester: Manchester University Press, pp. 26–44.

The EU as a community of practice: foreign policy communications in the COREU network

Federica Bicchi

ABSTRACT   This contribution shows the added value of analysing the European Union (EU), and more specifically the EU foreign policy system, as a community of practice, i.e. a group of people who routinely get together on a common or similar enterprise with the aim of developing and sharing practical knowledge. The paper analyses the COREU network, which allows member states and EU institutions to exchange confidential information about foreign policy. It argues that officials involved display the key features of a community of practice: (1) there is a high degree of mutual engagement; (2) the functions served by the network go well beyond what was first stipulated; (3) there is a shared repertoire of resources to negotiate meaning. The existence of such a community of practice suggests that there is in the EU foreign policy system at least one organizational structure able to transcend national boundaries and based instead on a European practice of foreign policy communications.

INTRODUCTION

The analysis of European Union (EU) foreign policy is currently in a paradoxical situation. It is attracting a lot of attention, but this is not resulting in an easy accumulation of academic knowledge; witness the debate on the nature of the EU's power (Manners 2002; Kagan 2003; Aggestam 2008; Hyde-Price 2008) or that on negotiations (Risse 2000; Deitelhoff and Müller 2005). One paradox is that intergovernmental accounts, while still widely used, are also widely criticized for not being able to capture a number of processes and situations, such as socialization (Checkel 2005). There is a feeling that we need to go 'beyond intergovernmentalism', although it is not clear how best we can do so. This contribution contributes to the attempt to go 'beyond intergovernmentalism' by suggesting that officials involved in EU foreign policy communications can be conceived as a 'community of practice', i.e., a group of people who routinely share a practice of communication and collective learning, and by doing so integrate different national systems and compensate for the qualitative discontinuities they bring to the EU foreign policy system.

The empirical evidence is provided by the COREU (*CORrespondence EUropéenne*) network, and the practice as well as the people that it involves.[1] Despite its relatively low status in the academic literature,[2] the network is 'the EU's foreign policy central nervous system' (Keukeleire and MacNaughtan 2008: 76), daily carrying communications about foreign policy to EU foreign policy actors. The volume of COREUs per year has been impressive. Member states and EU institutions have exchanged c. 40 messages per working day, although the number is much higher at peak times. The content of the messages is even more surprising. While initially confined to annotated agendas and minutes, they now include all stages of the policy cycle. Moreover, communication focuses not only on Common Foreign and Security Policy (CFSP), but also on member states' bilateral relations, thus further tying national foreign policies into the EU foreign policy system. The COREU network has thus established a communication practice and contributed to the creation of a community of practitioners who have developed a shared repertoire of resources for negotiating meaning (of international events, of their own role and identity, of key norms, etc.). Such a community involves not only the European Correspondents, who are the main referents for CFSP in national ministries of foreign affairs and EU institutions, but also a wider set of officials and diplomats, including Political Directors, who feed information into the network and benefit from its circulation.

The role of communication in European Political Communication (EPC)/ CFSP was first highlighted by Philippe de Schoutheete (1980), who suggested that the EU foreign policy system would move beyond being a '*communauté d'information*' to become a '*communauté de vue*' and eventually a '*communauté d'action*', based on trust and shared narratives. Developments along these lines have been marked, although not linear: representatives of member states and of EU institutions have become progressively enmeshed not only in face-to-face interactions in Brussels, as the 'Brusselization' literature suggests (e.g., Allen 1998), but also in a parallel thickening of the web of communications between capitals.

How are we to understand the meaning of such a thick set of communications between member states and EU institutions on matters of foreign policy? In particular, why do member states and EU institutions communicate so much via COREU and to what effect? This contribution aims to answer these questions by drawing on the concept of community of practice. I suggest that we can interpret the EU as a community of practice based on its practice of foreign policy communication. A community of practice is formed by a group of individuals who routinely get together on a common or similar enterprise with the aim of sharing practical knowledge and in the process create a common repertoire of resources (Seely-Brown and Duguid 1991; Wenger 1998; Adler 2008, 2010). A simple example would be people at home trying to repair a recalcitrant piece of equipment who join an internet discussion group to find out more about the task. If that discussion group becomes a routine resource to be used when faced with similar problems, individuals may acquire an additional identity layer as they exchange tips online with their newly acquired 'mates'. There are three elements to a community of practice: (1) the mutual engagement between individuals in their ongoing get-together on a joint enterprise; (2) the fact that individuals 'appropriate' the task and interpret it according to locally negotiated rules, rather than abstract manuals; (3) the common repertoire of rules and norms created in the process, which amount to shared practical knowledge. As will be shown, these elements have existed in the case of the EU foreign policy practice of communication via COREU.

This contribution will look first at the notion of community of practice and how it has been applied to the EU, before analysing COREU communication practice and the community that it has created.

THE EU AS A COMMUNITY OF PRACTICE

The concept of community of practice was first developed in the context of organizational studies and management as a contribution to organizational learning.[3] It has since migrated to (among other disciplines) international relations (IR), thanks to the work of Emanuel Adler (2008, 2010),[4] who first applied it to the EU.

The empirical basis for the concept lies in Julian Edgerton Orr's (1996) work on service technicians' work practices. He analysed how service technicians repairing photocopiers made sense of uncertain conditions, such as those encountered when an error code reported by a machine did not correspond to the actual error – something that should not occur according to the manuals. He showed how swapping stories about how to fix machines was central to the creation of a coherent account from unco-ordinated bits of information. This, according to John Seeley-Brown and Paul Duguid (1991), amounted to a community of practice composed of service technicians, whose identity was shaped by their professional practice.

Further elaborating on the definition of community of practice, Etienne Wenger (1998, 2000) identified three elements: (1) an ongoing mutual engagement; (2) a sense of joint enterprise; and (3) a shared repertoire. These are worth examining in depth because they lend themselves to being applied to communities of practice in the EU, along similar lines to those explored by Adler (2008, 2010).

First, members build their community through mutual engagement: '[t]hey interact with one another, establishing norms and relationships of *mutuality* that reflect these interactions' (Wenger 2000: 229, emphasis in the original). In other words, practices do not exist in the abstract. They exist because people are engaged in actions on an ongoing basis, to the point at which they develop into routines. Practices are thus to be understood as socially meaningful competent routine performances (Adler 2010: 68), which emerge as 'the result of inarticulate, practical knowledge that makes what is to be done appear "self-evident" or commonsensical' (Pouliot 2008: 258). Importantly, while based on a routine, a practice differs from a habit, as it does not merely lead to repetition.[5] The emphasis here is on the regularity of the pattern, which is more than a set of isolated rational decisions, but less than a completely passive habit. Furthermore, members sustain 'dense' relations of mutual engagement organized around what they are to do (Wenger 1998: 74) and practices are to be understood as 'social' practices (ibid.: 47). It is this ongoing and thick mutual engagement that constitutes the fabric of the community. The venue in which it develops depends on the task. It may, but does not necessarily, entail geographical proximity. In fact, in this era of 'network society' (Castells 1996), virtual communities are increasingly relevant.

Second, members are bound together by a sense of the joint enterprise involved in accomplishing a task. Not everybody has to agree on what the end goal is and how to reach it, but there must be a local, contextualized and indigenous response to the external stimulus. There needs to be a feeling of 'appropriated' enterprise (Cox 2005: 532), in which members re-interpret (and most likely distort) the will of the overarching institutional authority. A community of practice is thus a 'community of interpretation', within which 'the shared means for interpreting complex activity get formed, transformed, and transmitted' (Seeley-Brown and Duguid 1991: 47).[6]

The 'appropriated' nature of the enterprise matters to the analysis of EU foreign policy because it highlights the possibility of 'decoupling' organizational logic from local understanding. Whereas the organizational perspective might, for instance, rely on an intergovernmental view of European integration, local understanding might be more Europeanized. Moreover, by getting together to discuss and share expertise/knowledge of different problems, practitioners belonging to a community of practice create the outlines of a community rooted in their professional practice, despite the fact that they belong to different organizational settings which might prefer a more intergovernmental take on European integration. This mirrors the phenomenon highlighted by Ben Tonra (2001) in the case of EU external relations, in which intensified personal interactions contributed to the development of a sense of collective endeavour and group identification among those officials involved, which in turn fed into a collective European identification. The attachment to a joint enterprise in a community of practice does not, however, preclude or detract from an attachment to and identification with other communities of practice (e.g., at the national level).

Third, communities of practice create a shared repertoire of meaning, which helps them address uncertainty. 'Over time, the joint pursuit of an enterprise creates resources for negotiating meaning' (Wenger 1998: 82). Resources can be very different and include routines, tools, ways of doing things, words, stories and concepts. While they are partly reified, repertoires remain partly ambiguous and thus open-ended. This process is akin to that of 'structuring the unknown' described by Robert H. Waterman (1990: 41) and that of 'sensemaking' explored by Karl E. Weick (1995).[7] The repertoire of resources that is continuously created and re-enacted in a community of practice helps turn the unexpected into normality. There are several ways in which this can be done. The community of practice formed around the COREU network has not just produced meaning of immediate value for EU foreign policy, but it has also (and predominantly) created internal meaning among practitioners that in turn has supported meaning creation for EU foreign policy.

A community of practice is thus a group of people who routinely share a practice of communication and collective learning. The underpinnings of the three characteristics (i.e., mutual engagement, appropriateness and shared repertoire) are a domain, a community and a practice. As Adler puts it, communities of practice are 'a domain of knowledge that constitutes like-mindedness, a community of people that creates the social fabric of learning, and shared practices that embody the knowledge the community develops, shares and maintains' (Adler 2010: 68). The mutual engagement (together with the element of routine) and the sense of shared enterprise described above underpin the community, whereas the common repertoire embodies the practice in a specific domain. The relationship between practice and practising is one of 'mutual constitution' (Gherardi 2006: 221,108), as the community is constituted in the act of practising and vice versa.

Despite the apparent tension between a macro and micro approach to communities of practice, the two are not mutually exclusive. Adler's macro analysis focuses on the EU as a civilization. He argues that CFSP can in fact be interpreted as a set of practices (such as multilateralism, co-operative security, preventive diplomacy, political dialogues, etc.), as can the EU more generally, especially when considering it in the guise of a 'normative power' (Adler 2010). This contribution embraces a micro perspective but reaches similar conclusions. One can argue that the EU is a 'community of communities,' enshrining a multitude of communities of practices, based on different tasks and different knowledge. While the macro perspective looks at the big picture and at how communities of practice can ultimately be cumulative, the microanalysis shows the daily practice of practitioners belonging to a community of practice as they engage in communicating about EU foreign policy.

It is worth exploring here the analytical differences between communities of practice, networks and other communities based on knowledge (such as epistemic communities and security communities). In a network, 'actors are formally equal' as they have equal rights (Lavenex and Schimmelfennig 2009: 797), although there is a degree of institutionalization and thus also potentially of influence of power asymmetries. Moreover, networks tend to be defined along the lines of functional expertise, and the voluntary basis and the process-oriented nature of networks also chime well with the profile of communities of practice. However, there is a crucial difference in the attention devoted to the relationship between actors involved (e.g., individuals, units, 'nodes'). Some network approaches do not focus on the depth of the existing relationship and instead look at the network's shape at a specific point in time (Wallace 2000; Mérand et al. 2011). Therefore, in the case of transgovernmental networks, the empirical evidence taken into account is potentially very similar to that considered here[8] and the analysis also aims to go 'beyond intergovernmentalism'. But the route taken can have significant diversions and the thickness of the postulated social relationship can vary considerably. The cases of epistemic communities and security communities are more straightforward, as they can be considered communities of practice as long as the analytical focus is on the practice that underpins the community (Adler 2008: 199).

The added value of analysing the EU foreign policy system as a community of practice based on its communications is twofold. First, it grounds EU foreign policy co-operation in the ongoing practice of communication. From this perspective, the EU foreign policy system is first and foremost a routinized system of communication between practitioners, which sustains one or more communities of practice[9] producing common resources and knowledge. Second, it connects EU foreign policy analysis to the current interest in IR in practices (e.g., Pouliot 2008) and communication (e.g., Albert *et al.* 2008). In practical terms, this entails opening up the possibility to analyse the effects of communications and practices (and practices of communication in particular) on the quality of the interaction among European negotiators.

The following analysis is a preliminary step in that direction. I will start by briefly sketching the EU foreign policy communication system. I will then show how the three main characteristics of a community of practice (i.e., mutual engagement, appropriateness and shared repertoire) apply to the practice and to the group of practitioners involved in the COREU network. The analysis will make use of proxies, the main value of which will be illustrative rather than demonstrative. The level of officials' mutual engagement will be measured through the thickness of the communications carried by the network, as shown both by their quantity and by the network's structure. The local appropriation of the task will be measured by the type and nature of documents carried by the network, which go well beyond codified 'best practice'. Finally, the existence of a common repertoire of rules and norms will be assessed, also *a contrario*, by analysing the impact on new members of joining the network.

THE EU FOREIGN POLICY COMMUNICATION SYSTEM

We can roughly categorize EU foreign policy communications according to inclusiveness and format. Inclusiveness refers to the actors involved in the communication structure. Communications can either involve all participants, or just a sub-set. The focus in this contribution is exclusively on the multilateral level (i.e. 27 member states and EU institutions). The format of communication can be either face-to-face or virtual. The first format is best exemplified by the constant stream of meetings, at various levels of the hierarchy and on a very broad range of topics, taking place in Brussels and in capitals on EU foreign affairs. European Correspondents, for instance, meet regularly in Brussels and in capitals at the margins of the Foreign Affairs Council meetings and of meetings of Political Directors. In parallel with face-to-face meetings, representatives of member states and EU institutions continue to communicate via a variety of virtual networks. The focus of this contribution is on the most important of these virtual networks, the COREU network, which carries communications related to CFSP. This is the oldest communication network in EU foreign policy and although other communication channels have emerged in the last few years, the COREU network has been crucial to the development of CFSP as we know it.[10]

A PRACTICE OF MUTUAL ENGAGEMENT

The quantity of communications going through the COREU network and its structure underscore the practice of mutual engagement between officials involved. The term COREU (which derives from *CORrespondence EUropéenne*) refers to the messages exchanged within a network of predefined actors. Technically speaking, it can be equated to a sophisticated telex system using encrypted transmission with dedicated terminals. Since its creation in 1973, the number of COREUs has continued to increase until recently (see Figure 1). While the introduction of CFSP brought a quantitative leap forward, the upwards trend continued, though at a slower pace, reaching a peak first in 1995 and then again in 2002. There are now grounds to believe that an equilibrium may be approached, but the impact of the creation of the European External Action Service (EEAS) will have to be taken into account before any firm conclusions on its level can be reached.[11] There is, therefore, a very thick daily practice of communication on matters of foreign policy among representatives of member states and EU institutions.

There are three traditional categories of CFSP actors sending and receiving COREUs:

(1) Member states, of which the Presidency used to play a particularly active role. More specifically, the COREU network links the 27 European Correspondents in member states' capitals, as well as the 27 Permanent Representatives in Brussels as passive recipients.
(2) The General Secretariat of the Council (GSC), which is the logistical backbone of the entire system.[12]
(3) The Commission, and more precisely the European Correspondent, which was located in the Directorate-General for External Relations (DG Relex 1A), while delegations in third countries have been passive recipients.[13]

Figure 1 Number of COREUs, by year
Source: Data provided by the GSC.

(4) The EEAS, which is bound to become the main originator of messages because of its cumulation of functions.

The system is configured as a 'hub and spoke', with the EEAS at its centre.[14] While the EEAS is connected to all participants, all other participants are connected only to the EEAS. While there is no room here to go into the technicalities of the system,[15] what matters for the purpose of this contribution is that this is a multilateral structure mediated by the EEAS/GSC hub, which acts as a guarantee that all communications are official and reach all participants. The system works by 'joining up' existing national and EU communication networks at a single point of contact (the European Correspondent) for each actor. Beyond that, communications are delegated to in-house channels, which allow the document sent by COREU to circulate according to local rules in the 27 ministries of foreign affairs, the EEAS, the GSC and the Commission. The same structure applies to incoming messages, in reverse order. To reach representatives of other member states and of EU institutions, officials send documents via their national networks to their European Correspondent, who then circulates them via COREU (and thus via the EEAS/GSC hub) to all other participants in the network. Centralization at dedicated points thus acts as an extra check that documents have the capitals' full backing and that only official positions are circulated. Moreover, having just one point of contact per member state (and in-house communication lines after that) makes for an agile and streamlined system.

The COREU system is biased in favour of horizontal multilateralism. As a rule, messages are addressed to all participants in the system. Exceptionally, bilateral COREUs may be used to connect the EEAS and the GSC, or the EEAS and one member state (for instance when a special report is due). The system thus works against the fragmentation of discussion into sub-groups. Its rationale is multilateral and encompassing, although proposals for reform currently suggest complementing it with communications involving just some actors and communications at different levels of the hierarchy.[16]

To what extent are practitioners all equally relevant to the community's practice? Pre-Lisbon, the GSC was on average the main originator of messages in the last decade, sending c. 20 per cent of all messages, because of its institutional responsibilities,[17] while Presidencies were the next most prolific, sending on average 10 per cent of messages. As the EEAS has incorporated both functions as well as the relevant part of the Commission, it is bound to become the main sender of COREUs and thus a crucial actor in circulation of information: how pivotal, however, remains to be seen as the practice develops. Moreover, some member states are more prone to send messages than others. As is to be expected, big member states (France, Germany, the United Kingdom) are the biggest originators, sending on average 6–7 per cent of messages. Interestingly, though, size is not all. Some smaller member states (the Netherlands and Sweden) are particularly active, whereas others (Italy and Spain) less so. Overall, it is remarkable how similar in quantity are the contributions that member states provide.[18]

The numbers of COREUs and the structure of the network thus reveal the extent of practitioners' mutual engagement in this common practice, which was particularly strong during the 1990s and the early 2000s, but which remains crucial today. Moreover, while some participants are more active than others, the structure of the system guarantees not only that all participants have a chance to participate actively, but also that they are all part of the vast majority of communications.

AN 'APPROPRIATED' TASK

Even more striking is the substance of COREUs exchanged, which shows the breadth of co-operation on matters of foreign policy and, more generally, the extent to which practitioners have 'appropriated' communications in EU foreign policy and 'decoupled' them from the official script.

In its original formulation, the COREU system was expected to ease the flow of information between participants prior to and after meetings. Prior to meetings, participants would exchange not only logistical details, but also comments on preliminary issues such as the agenda. After meetings, minutes would be circulated and loose threads tightened. The more contemporary formal document on the subject, the *CFSP Guide* (Council of the European Union 2008), reflects a limited evolution of the role of the COREU. The most 'appropriate' ways of using the system are at 'the stage of the initiative and prior reactions' and 'for the records of working party discussions', while 'the preparation of documents by COREU is to be discouraged' (ibid.: 33). In exceptional circumstances the system may be used for taking decisions and finalizing documents, depending on the urgency of the matter.

This description, however, does not capture the practice and the nature of full-range consultations now taking place between member states via COREU. The expansion of the COREU's role has occurred in two directions (Figure 2). First, it has spanned the entire policy cycle, including decision-making. Second, COREU has transcended the national/European barrier (although with the notable exception of decision-making and with two-way traffic only at the agenda-setting level).

Going full cycle: the COREU system across policy stages

Agenda-setting has been a staple function of the COREU system. The discussion in CFSP starts with the EEAS (previously the Presidency) circulating a draft agenda for discussion at the next meeting of the relevant formation within the Council's hierarchy. Other participants, and especially national representatives, respond with comments, beginning a 'virtual discussion' about the various points. As a consequence, representatives of member states and EU institutions routinely come to the negotiation table with a very good understanding of each other's positions, though obviously built on other sources as well (bilateral meetings, etc.).

Stage in the policy cycle Level	Agenda-setting	Policy formulation	Decision-making	Implementation
CFSP	COREUs (agendas)	→	→ COREUs (minutes, silent assent) →	
National foreign policies	↕	↕		↕

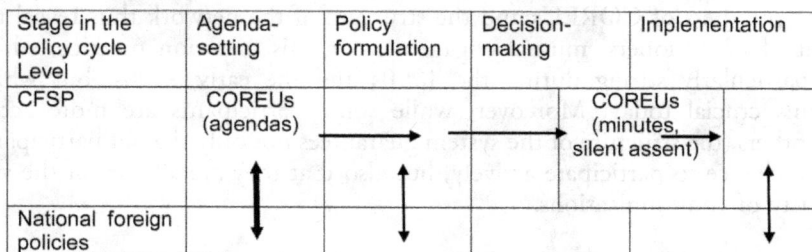

Figure 2 The expansion of the COREU system

These 'virtual' exchanges via COREU on the agenda tend to shift into policy formulation, as documents highlighting policy options are also circulated and commented upon. In this respect, the most relevant type of privileged information going through the COREU are political reports, most notably reports by Heads of Missions (HoMs) and by EU Special Representatives (EUSRs). HoMs reports on human rights are, for instance, routinely circulated, particularly prior to co-operation or association councils, when issues of democracy and human rights might be addressed. In the case of negotiations and/or crises, HoMs or EUSR reports, including political analyses of facts and options for action, are circulated.[19]

The COREU system has also made inroads into the decision-making stage, via the simplified written procedure.[20] This procedure requires that if a document, marked for silent assent, does not raise objections by member states within the specified deadline, it is considered approved.[21] Technically speaking, the written procedure for the formal adoption of acts in the Council (across all policy areas) requires a formal answer from member states. However the 'informal' or simplified written procedure works on the assumption that only member states willing to object to the proposed text will make their voices heard. The deadline can be as short as two hours from the sending of the text. The procedure reflects the need to react quickly to international events, but also the desire to avoid unnecessary discussions during meetings. It is difficult to quantify the number of times it is used, given the secrecy surrounding the COREU system. Interviewees suggest that the silence procedure is routine for at least all CFSP declarations issued by the EU, as well as for a number of other acts that are considered more administrative in nature, such as extensions of EUSR mandates.[22]

A written procedure via COREU changes the nature of the decision-making game, because it has a built-in bias against objections.[23] In most cases a small number of member states do ask for changes to the proposed text, but a policy of 'self-restriction' applies to minor, non-red line changes.[24] Some of the issues might be postponed to a later discussion in the working groups or in the Political and Security Committee (PSC). But member states do not like to be (and to be seen as) the first to break the silent assent process.[25] In fact, it is considered a 'most useful' instrument for coming to an agreement.[26] Therefore, contrary to what the *CFSP Guide* suggests, there is a routine element to the use of the silent assent procedure, especially at the lower end of the CFSP instruments' spectrum, subordinating national foreign policies to CFSP on ordinary (non-red line) issues.

Finally, the exchange of information via COREU can also sustain the creation and implementation of policies going beyond the very limited function of minutes. This is the case of arms' denials. The EU approved a Code of Conduct for Arms Exports in 1998, laying down criteria for the harmonization of practices, while leaving member states free to decide whether to grant or deny applications for licences to export arms. The Code is politically, though not legally, binding (Bauer and Bromley 2004: 2). Member states have agreed to circulate details of licences refused together with an explanation for their refusal through COREU.[27] Before any member state grants a licence previously denied by another member state for an essentially identical transaction within the last three years, it needs to consult the member state which issued the denial. This practice has brought transparency to the EU's arms exports system, increased the coherence of member states' actions and, most importantly, created a *de facto* common policy based on the common practice of circulating information via COREU.

The practice of consultation via COREU is thus occurring at all stages in the policy cycle, as member states and EU institutions formulate and implement decisions via what is a (sophisticated) fax machinery. This is particularly true when it comes to less politically salient issues, but the same principle also applies to co-operation among departments inside national ministries of foreign affairs. The relevant point here is the built-in tendency of the system to expand beyond its formal limits, which suggests that practitioners are finding it more useful than as originally codified – and they are offering a local interpretation of how the system should be used.

Eroding the national/European frontier: bilateral relations via a multilateral framework

The second direction in which the COREU system has evolved is towards the progressive erosion of the distinction between the European and the national levels. Member states feed into the system issues beyond the remit of CFSP/ Title V, and they use the information gathered within the CFSP framework for national purposes. National foreign policies are thus becoming embedded into an EU foreign policy system of communications, as shown by the links between the two levels, covering most policy stages (Figure 2).

Member states have acquired the practice of informing each other of bilateral consultations at the ministerial level with third countries or groups of countries. This is a relatively 'easy' way of fulfilling their obligations to 'inform and consult',[28] but it has far-reaching consequences. Interviewees reported several examples of how a short and bland report offers other member states the opportunity to ask for further details at a (generally bilateral) meeting, especially if there is mention of contentious dossiers such as migration or energy.[29]

However, member states do not report on all the activities of their ministers of foreign affairs, and the variation in information provided is broad. On average, interviewees estimate that roughly 50 per cent of bilateral relations are reported via COREU.[30] Moreover, the information provided can be selected for strategic reasons. Meetings in which member states stressed a European position are widely reported and so are meetings that support the national position of the sending member state. More sensitive information may be omitted. Still, the effects of this practice are to open up national foreign policies to close scrutiny by other member states, to foster trust and communication, and thus to strengthen the foundations of the community of practice.

Moreover, the relationship between COREUs and national foreign policy also works in the other direction, as some categories of COREUs pertaining to CFSP can affect national preferences. HoMs and EUSRs reports, for instance, contain assessments of developments on the ground. As the vast majority of member states have embassies in less than one-third of the globe (Keukeleire and Mac-Naughtan 2008: 134), this information is read with interest and COREUs are considered a 'very useful way' to keep updated.[31] Similarly, the implementation of co-ordination of the denial of arms, while leaving member states fully responsible for the decision to grant or deny arms licences (and to report to other member states about their conduct), has been based on the circulation of information via COREU. Importantly, even though they do not report the totality of their bilateral actions, member states feel the political obligation to report, thus showing that the system has acquired a momentum of its own.

A COMMON REPERTOIRE OF SHARED KNOWLEDGE

Officials using the COREU network form a community of practice for a third reason (alongside the routine of mutual engagement and the sense of joint enterprise), namely that a common repertoire of shared knowledge has developed. Resources included in the repertoire can be (and are) very different, as they range from routines and ways of doing things to words, concepts and stories (Wenger 1998: 82). In the case of the community of practice under scrutiny, resources do not all have a direct impact on the construction of meaning for EU foreign policy, but they do reduce uncertainty about communication and can contribute to sense-making in EU foreign policy.

First, linking into the COREU network is a 'rite of passage' and has a profound effect on new members. Karolina Pomorska (2007) shows this in the case of Poland. Before the Eastern enlargement, all candidate countries were linked to the Association Countries Network, which allowed them to see draft positions in advance of publication, thus helping to co-ordinate national declarations. This gave Polish officials some sense of how short the deadlines could be. But nothing prepared them for what was to come: as the COREU system kicked in on the first day of Poland's full participation, diplomats experienced 'a shock' as the number of COREUs received amounted to 100. The distribution of documents was initially done 'physically by officials running around the ministerial building' (Pomorska 2007: 38), but the outcome was chaos and disruption. As a result, procedures were changed significantly, new technological means introduced, and more generally a new 'way of doing things' was established. Polish officials learned a new practice, which came to affect their identity. At the same time, they have become part of a community that they themselves constitute through their participation. Something similar occurred in other cases of enlargement, such as Spain (Gillespie 1995: 115–17).[32]

Second, intensive communication via COREU contributes to the creation of a common language and a common knowledge. The ongoing traffic has progressively established a set of joint expressions capturing the EU's role and working method: 'fact-finding mission', 'election observation', 'political dialogue', among others, are codes with a specific meaning that practitioners have come to recognize as part of their daily routine and of their understanding of what the EU is about.[33] Moreover, communication via COREU can also be central to the construction of a common knowledge. HoMs reports are a good example. They are prepared jointly by the Heads of Mission of member states in a third country together with the Head of the EU Delegation. These reports are generally requested either by a working group or by the PSC. They contribute to 'structure the unknown' and create common resources. As recounted in an interview,[34] a small member state was holding the Presidency, when faced with the necessity to 'do something' about a Latin American country in the EU context. However, this specific country did not have an embassy in that county and the facts were unclear. Diplomats from that small country involved in CFSP thus informally decided that their representative chairing the relevant working group would ask for a HoMs report, which national representatives on the ground would provide, as a 'first stab' at the process of drafting an EU response. Faced with uncertainty and the unavailability of 'traditional' national channels, officials thus turned to the COREU network and to the practice of HoMs reporting. Several HoMs reports have in fact acquired a semi-automatic character and are prepared on a regular basis.

This does not mean that COREU equals consensus. Breakdowns of virtual communications happen, as shown not only by the notorious ill-fated attempt of the Irish Presidency to agree by COREU on a declaration responding to the Soviet invasion of Afghanistan in 1979 (Nuttall 1992: 154), but also by a more recent attempt by the EEAS to craft a highly political declaration by simplified written procedure, which had to be called off.[35] Face-to-face interactions retain their usefulness as the increasing number of meetings in Brussels testifies. The point here is that in parallel with and complementing meetings, officials working on CFSP and connected by COREU have developed a shared repertoire of practices, which help make sense of reality 'out there'.

CONCLUSIONS

This contribution has shown that EU foreign policy communications via COREU have established a community of practice involving representatives of member states and EU institutions, which has been able to transcend national boundaries and recompose national differences into a common European practice of communication. Its existence has been illustrated by the three elements characterizing communities of practice (Wenger 1998). First, the traffic and the structure of the COREU network point to the high level of sustained engagement on the part of practitioners in the communication practice. Second, the 'decoupling' of local practice from institutionally codified best practice, as shown in the widespread use of COREUs across the policy cycle and for national purposes too, testifies to the extent to which this community of practice has been able to 'appropriate' the task beyond official guidelines. Third, despite the limits imposed by COREU secrecy, it is possible to suggest that practitioners involved in the COREU network have not only created a common language and repertoire of resources, as shown by the difficulties encountered at first by newcomers, but have also made it possible to establish common resources for sense-making, as in HoMs reports. Although there is a formal institutional overarching framework, represented by the EU or more specifically in our case the EU foreign policy system, the practical value of the COREU system is represented by practitioners coming together from different organizations to discuss, share and establish expertise and knowledge – and in the process, creating a community rooted in their professional practice.

The added value of such an analysis lies in the fact that it shows how the EU can be considered to have gone 'beyond intergovernmentalism'. While 'red lines' continue to exist and delimit a strictly intergovernmental arena, much of the daily practice occurs outside 'red lines'. In this realm, the existence of a community of practice based on the COREU network underscores how the gap between self-contained national polities can be and has been bridged by officials who in their daily activities support the weaving together of a common cognitive framework. Professional practice acquires a routinized element and becomes part of the 'identity work' of diplomats. In the daily, 'non-red lines' practice, the COREU communication practice thus contributes to dilute the 'purely national' character of foreign policies by tightening relations between officials belonging to different countries and by nurturing a joint cognitive and social system for policy-making.

The extent to which this one has developed into a supranational community of practice (Adler 2010: 74) remains to be explored, as does the potential number, contours and dynamics of communities involved in the EU foreign policy system. The specific consequences of communities of practices in terms of decision-making, for instance, would need to be investigated more in detail. The COREU network can be considered a hard case, given that it is largely based on virtual communications. It might also be a case that has passed its peak, given the recent weakening of the communication practice. We can expect the intersubjective relationship to be even stronger in a face-to-face context, such as the PSC Ambassadors and working group representatives in the Council, where the practice of mutual engagement is particularly developed. In fact, a thickening practice in Brussels, together with other concomitant factors, might detract from the COREU traffic and practice, as new communities of practice emerge and take over from the one analysed here.

Biographical note: Dr Federica Bicchi is Lecturer at the Department of International Relations at London School of Economics and Political Science.

ACKNOWLEDGEMENTS

I am very grateful to Helene Sjursen, Ben Tonra, Stephan Stetter, Kirsten Ainley and the reviewers for comments, as well as to the participants in two seminars organized by ARENA in Oslo in September and October 2010, and in the workshop organized by the University of Maastricht in November 2010. I am also grateful to Lucia Garcia who pointed me in the direction of communities of practice and to Caterina Carta for assisting in the research for this paper.

This contribution emanates from RECON (Reconstituting Democracy in Europe), an Integrated Project supported by the European Commission's Sixth Framework Programme.

NOTES

1 The technical name of the network is CORTESY (acronym of *COREU Terminal System*). This contribution is based on data obtained from the General Secretariat of the Council and on 16 interviews with practitioners directly involved in the running of the system. Given the confidentiality of the network, extra care has been taken here to protect their identities.
2 For an exception, see Dijkstra and Vanhoonacker (2011).
3 See Cox (2005) and Gherardi (2000).
4 See also Bremberg (2010).
5 Gherardi (2000: 214) based on Polanyi (1958/1962).
6 The level of 'subversiveness' embodied by communities of practice is a matter of discussion. In his subsequent work with McDermott and Snyder (2002), Wenger emphasized informal groups and the sharing of an interest. This seems to downplay the role of power, especially in larger organizations. But analyses of communities of practice could equally apply to ongoing power struggles within hierarchies (Hughes *et al.* 2007: 9–11).
7 Weick (1995: 91–100) distinguishes between ambiguity and uncertainty. In both cases, sense-making entails the invention of sense that precedes the interpretation of events.

8 Mérand *et al.* (2011: 127) define co-operation as 'intensive exchange of important information and joint work towards the development of common positions'.
9 And potentially more than one, although the focus here is on the one based on the COREU network.
10 Another virtual network, not analysed here, is ESDP-net (see Duke 2006).
11 For interpretations of this partial decline, see Bicchi and Carta (2010).
12 The GSC has remained linked to the system also because of its administrative responsibilities in relation to the CFSP.
13 Via the Commission's internal network.
14 Technically, though, the GSC is at the centre, as it manages the system, while in terms of content it is the EEAS that is at the centre.
15 See Bicchi and Carta (2010).
16 The proposal, which goes under the acronym of SESAME (Secure European System for Applications in a Multi-vendor Environment), has been on the agenda since 2001, but conflicting national interests have complicated, and probably stalled, the discussion.
17 On this, see Bátora (2008: 240).
18 For specific figures, see Bicchi and Carta (2010).
19 Interview with senior EU official, December 2010. For a caveat about sources, see Note 2.
20 See *Council's rules of procedure*, Article 12(4), OJEC L106/29, 15 April 2004.
21 The procedure can also be used for the approval of internal documents such as agendas.
22 Interview with senior EU official, December 2010; with national representative, July 2010; written interview with senior official, GSC, July 2010.
23 See Aus (2008: 113) and Lewis (2008: 175), for an analysis of the written procedure in the European Communities context.
24 Interview with national representative, April 2010.
25 Interview with national representative, June 2010.
26 Interview with national representative, April 2010.
27 They also publish an annual report, which contributes to increased transparency. See Bauer and Bromley (2004).
28 Interview with national representative, June 2010.
29 Interview with national representative, November 2009; national representative, April 2010; national representative, June 2010; national representative, July 2010.
30 Interview with national representative, May 2010.
31 Interview with national representative, March 2011.
32 See also examples in Hocking and Spence (2002).
33 Interview with EU official, November 2010.
34 Interview with national representative, June 2010.
35 Interview with national representative, March 2011.
36 While Cross (2006) suggests that European diplomats represent a single community, Spence (2009) suggests that there is a community of more European-oriented and one of more national-oriented diplomats.

REFERENCES

Adler, E. (2008) 'The spread of security communities: communities of practice, self-restraint, and NATO's post-Cold War transformation', *European Journal of International Relations* 14(20): 195–230.
Adler, E. (2010) 'Europe as a civilizational community of practice', in P.J. Katzenstein (ed.), *Civilizations in World Politics: Plural and Pluralist Perspectives*, Abingdon: Routledge, pp. 67–90.

Aggestam, L. (2008) 'Introduction: ethical power Europe?', *International Affairs* 84(1): 1–11.

Albert, M., Kessler, O. and Stetter, S. (2008) 'On order and conflict: international relations and the "communicative turn"', *Review of International Studies* 34(S1): 43–67.

Allen, D. (1998) '"Who speaks for Europe?" The search for an effective and coherent external policy', in J. Peterson and H. Sjursen (eds), *A Common Foreign Policy for Europe? Competing Visions of the CFSP*, London: Routledge, pp. 41–58.

Aus, J. (2008) 'The mechanisms of consensus: coming to agreement on Community asylum policy', in D. Naurin and H. Wallace (eds), *Unveiling the Council of the European Union. Games Governments Play in Brussels*, New York: Palgrave Macmillan.

Bátora, J. (2008) 'Collusions and collisions in organizing diplomacy in the EU', in U. Sverdrup and J. Trondal (eds), *The Organizational Dimension of Politics. Essays in Honour of Morten Egeberg*, Bergen: Fagbokforlaget.

Bauer, S. and Bromley, M. (2004) 'The European Union Code of Conduct on Arms Exports', *SIPRI Policy Paper 8*, Stockholm: Stockholm International Peace Research Institute.

Bicchi, F. and Carta, C. (2010) 'The COREU/CORTESY network and the circulation of information within EU foreign policy', *RECON Online Working Paper 2010/01*, Oslo: ARENA.

Bremberg, N. (2010) 'Security, governance and community beyond the European Union: exploring issue-level dynamics in Euro-Mediterranean civil protection', *Mediterranean Politics* 15(2): 169–88.

Castells, M. (1996) *The Rise of the Network Society*, Cambridge, MA: Blackwell.

Checkel, J. (2005) 'International institutions and socialization in Europe: introduction and framework', *International Organization* 59(4): 801–26.

Council of the European Union (2008) '"CFSP Guide" – compilation of relevant texts', 10898/08, Brussels, 18 June.

Cox, A. (2005) 'What are communities of practice? A comparative review of four seminal works', *Journal of Information Science* 31(6): 527–40.

Cross, M. (2006) *The European Diplomatic Corps*, Basingstoke: Palgrave.

de Schoutheete, P. (1980) *La Coopération Politique Européenne*, Paris and Brussels: Nathan/Labor.

Deitelhoff, N. and Müller, H. (2005) 'Theoretical paradise – empirically lost? Arguing with Habermas', *Review of International Studies* 31(1): 167–79.

Dijkstra, H. and Vanhoonacker, S. (2011) 'The changing politics of information in European foreign policy', *Journal of European Integration*, 33(5): 541–58.

Duke, S. (2006) 'Intelligence, security and information flows in CFSP', *Intelligence and National Security* 21(4): 604–30.

Gherardi, S. (2000) 'Practice-based theorizing on learning and knowing in organizations', *Organization* 7(2): 211–23.

Gherardi, S. (2006) *Organizational Knowledge: The texture of Workplace Learning*, Oxford: Blackwell Publishing.

Gillespie, R. (1995) *Democratic Spain. Reshaping External Relations in a Changing World*, London: Routledge.

Hocking, B. and Spence, D. (eds) (2002) *Foreign Ministries in the European Union. Integrating Diplomats*, Basingstoke: Palgrave.

Hughes, J., Jewson, N. and Unwin, L. (2007) 'Introduction', in J. Hughes, N. Jewson and L. Unwin (eds), *Communities of Practice. Critical Perspectives*, Abingdon and New York: Routledge.

Hyde-Price, A. (2008) 'A "tragic actor"? A realist perspective on "ethical power Europe"', *International Affairs* 84(1): 29–44.

Kagan, R. (2003) *Of Paradise and Power. America and Europe in the New World Order*, New York: A. Knopf.

Keukeleire, S. and MacNaughtan, J. (2008) *The Foreign Policy of the European Union*, Basingstoke: Palgrave.

Lavenex, S. and Schimmelfennig, F. (2009) 'EU rules beyond EU borders: theorizing external governance in European politics', *Journal of European Public Policy* 16(6): 791–812.

Lewis, J. (2008) 'Strategic bargaining, norms and deliberation', in D. Naurin and H. Wallace (eds), *Unveiling the Council of the European Union. Games Governments Play in Brussels*, New York: Palgrave Macmillan.

Manners, I. (2002) 'Normative power Europe: a contradiction in terms?', *Journal of Common Market Studies* 40(2): 235–58.

Mérand, F., Hofmann, S. and Irondelle, B. (2011) 'Governance and state power: a network analysis of European security', *Journal of Common Market Studies* 49(1): 121–47.

Nuttall, S.J. (1992) *European Political Cooperation*, Oxford: Clarendon Press.

Orr, J.E. (1996) *Talking about Machines. An Ethnography of a Modern Job*, Ithaca, NY: Cornell University Press.

Polanyi, M. (1958/1962) *Personal Knowledge. Towards a Post-critical Philosophy*, London: Routledge.

Pomorska, K. (2007) 'the impact of enlargement: Europeanization of Polish foreign policy?', *The Hague Journal of Diplomacy* 2(1): 25–51.

Pouliot, V. (2008) 'The logic of practicality: a theory of practice of security communities', *International Organization* 62(2): 257–88.

Risse, T. (2000) '"Let's argue!": communicative action in world politics', *International Organization* 54(1): 1–39.

Seeley-Brown, J. and Duguid, P. (1991) 'Organizational learning and communities of practice', *Organization Science* 2(1): 40–57.

Spence, D. (2009) 'Taking stock: 50 years of European diplomacy', *The Hague Journal of Diplomacy* 4(2): 235–59.

Tonra, B. (2001) *The Europeanisation of National Foreign Policy. Dutch, Danish and Irish Foreign Policy in the European Union*, Aldershot: Ashgate.

Wallace, H. (2000) 'The institutional setting: five variations on a theme', in H. Wallace and W. Wallace (eds), *Policy-making in the European Union*, 4th edn, Oxford and New York: Oxford University Press.

Waterman, R.H. (1990) *Adhocracy. The Power to Change*, Memphis, TN: Whittle Direct Books.

Weick, K.E. (1995) *Sensemaking in Organizations*, Thousand Oaks, CA: Sage.

Wenger, E. (1998) *Communities of Practice*, Cambridge, MA: Cambridge University Press.

Wenger, E. (2000) 'Communities of practice and social learning systems', *Organization* 7(2): 225–46.

Wenger, E., McDermott, R. and Snyder, W.M. (2002) *A Guide to Managing Knowledge. Cultivating Communities of Practice*, Boston, MA: Harvard Business School Press.

The political theory and practice of parliamentary participation in the Common Security and Defence Policy

Christopher Lord

ABSTRACT   This contribution develops normative arguments for the democratic and parliamentary control of the Common Security and Defence Policy (CSDP). However, on the Kantian assumption that 'ought implies can', it also tries to make a case for parliamentary control in the face of scepticism about parliamentary politics in general, the capacities of the European Parliament (EP) and national parliaments to exercise satisfactory levels of public control over Union decisions, and the participation of parliaments in security decisions.

INTRODUCTION

Proposals for new security initiatives have followed hard on the heels of one another since the end of the 1990s. Attention seems to switch between initiatives, solutions seem to chase problems as well as vice versa (Cohen *et al.* 1972), and those things that are unplanned sometimes seem to be more consequential than those that are carefully designed. As Christopher Hill (2003: 292–7) has observed, there is something problematic about the notion that actors altogether *choose* their foreign and security policies. The Common Security and Defence Policy (CSDP) seems no exception. Individual security missions often respond to unforeseen events. Long-term collaboration in the development of security capabilities may require large but precarious guesses about the future.

Thus, both short- and long-term considerations seem to limit the rationality and intentionality of decisions. That might, in turn, suggest that CSDP is not a fruitful area for democratic control, given that the latter presupposes that outcomes can, indeed, be controlled.

Against that view, this contribution uses democratic theory to identify what it is about the CSDP that may require its democratic control, in part by parliamentary means. Beyond what is needed to make that argument it does not attempt an exhaustive analysis of existing institutional arrangements. Even where it turns to questions of feasibility, it does so only to anticipate a specifically philosophical objection: namely, that 'ought implies can' in any non-utopian world. Yet, as this last point implies, the essay has a practical purpose. By clarifying what various philosophical questions of democratic theory might mean for the CSDP the paper also aims to reach a better understanding of some of the legitimation issues involved in its institutional design. In setting out this agenda, I make no apology for proceeding pedantically. The next section develops five arguments for the democratic control of the CSDP. The section after that gives reasons why that control may need to take a parliamentary form, and the final section considers how the normative case for greater parliamentary control of the CSDP might stand up to practical constraints on its realization.

DEMOCRATIC CONTROL?

Justifications for democracy are of two kinds (Weale 1999). Intrinsic justifications hold that democracy is desirable in and of itself, since it amounts to a form of autonomy in which the people can see themselves as authoring their own decisions directly or through representatives. Put another way, it 'is that set of institutions by which individuals are empowered as free and equal citizens to form and change the terms of their common life together' (Bohman 2007: 66). Consequential justifications, on the other hand, hold that democracy is not so much justified by its inherent qualities as by its likely effects. Thus, it has been variously claimed that democracies are more likely to maintain peaceful international relations, to sustain higher levels of economic and social development, to satisfy the needs of the governed, and to offer rights protections and guarantees against arbitrary government (Pettit 1997). Given these justifications it is possible to identify five reasons as follows why security co-ordination at the European level should be democratically controlled.

European security co-ordination will lead to legally enforced obligations

If it follows from 'intrinsic' justifications that citizens in a democracy should be able to see themselves as authoring their own laws through representatives (Habermas 1996: 38, 171–72), it matters that sooner or later European security co-ordination will have to be paid for by taxes that individuals are legally obliged to pay; that sooner or later individual troops will have to meet their legal obligations to obey orders, to fight when told to do so, and to spend time in dangerous or uncongenial parts of the world, all under the *aegis* of European security missions.

Of course, such legally enforced obligations will be experienced by individuals through the medium of national law. However, the origin of those obligations in European Union (EU)-level co-ordinations can be expected to be visible, especially in the case of troops deployed in multinational forces that describe themselves as EU security missions, which fly EU flags and receive their orders from more or less co-ordinated commands attempting to carry out mandates agreed by the European Council. Where, moreover, governments and sections of the media allow the European Union to absorb a part of the blame for unwelcome consequences of decisions that have in fact been agreed by national authorities, they should not be overly surprised if public opinion attributes to the European Union a role in shaping the legal obligations that sustain security co-ordination at the European level. Nor in a sense would those attributions be wrong. In so far as they feel a need to maintain the credibility and mutual reciprocity of European security co-operation, national authors of 'hard law' may feel themselves constrained by a 'soft law' of security agreements concluded at the European level. We will return to this point.

European Union security co-ordination will be redistributive of values, and entail fundamental normative choices

Sometimes it is possible to act collectively without redistributing values at all, or even without choosing between alternatives that distribute gains from co-operation in different ways. Decisions of this kind are no more than technical solutions to pure co-ordination problems. They merely help co-ordinate mutually advantageous behaviours between actors whose values are not in conflict. Under such conditions, neither intrinsic nor consequential considerations seem to require democratic control. Pure co-ordinations do not raise the problem of how to secure the agreements of individuals to laws by which they are themselves coerced, since they do not in any meaningful sense compel people to do what they would rather not do. And, since they do not re-distribute values at all, they imply no risk that arbitrary choices will be made between values (Buchanan and Tullock 1962).

Could European security co-operation amount to a purely technical co-ordination of actor preferences? I doubt it. It will always be possible to argue that the resources committed to particular security initiatives could have been used elsewhere. Such conflicts of priority are likely to be acute the more resources are limited, the more dangers there are to be confronted, the more they arrive at the same time, the greater the differences between member states in the degree to which they are likely to be affected by different dangers, and the less Europeans can sit back and leave the management of their security to others.

Above all, the development of a security policy begs the questions of what values and identities it is intended to defend (Waever 1996), and of what rights conceptions it should observe. The point about rights needs labouring since it is often misunderstood and misrepresented. It has no necessary connection to imposing European rights conceptions on others. It does not presuppose universal rights exist or even that Europeans are agreed amongst themselves on the nature of rights. Rather, rights conceptions will shape and constrain what can be achieved within a security co-ordination even in so far as individual parties to that co-ordination feel obliged to follow *their own* beliefs about the rights of others in *their own* behaviour.

Much has been written on what ought to be the normative-basis of the Union's behaviour towards its outside world. Debates about the feasibility and desirability of it developing as a military, civilian (Duchêne 1972) or normative power (Manners 2002) need not be repeated here. Nor need a great deal be said to demonstrate that these categories are, in any case, interconnected. Military power requires normative justification if it is to be more than repression or naked force, and normative power supposes *justifiable* coercion if it is to be more than normative example. It is likewise hard to see how even an international actor with a 'civilian-power bias' could avoid some coercive enforcement of norms. Trade sanctions – which are presumably civilian instruments – can, as we know, be very coercive indeed. Attempts to confine security roles to the civilian power end of the spectrum by restricting them to peacekeeping and to the reconstruction of post-conflict societies would at the very least involve the Union adopting the role of credible enforcer of norms negotiated with parties to the peace.

In sum, then, alternative conceptions of the Union's international and security roles converge more than is always acknowledged on behaviours that are all likely to involve some admixture of power, coercion, choices of value and rights conceptions. But if that is so, then those policies must be covered by the argument that democratic legitimacy is the only form of legitimacy available to liberal societies (Rawls 1993: 38). Since those societies are committed to regarding individuals as morally autonomous agents who are equally entitled to judge for themselves what is good and right, they must also be committed to the belief that citizens should be able to control all collective decisions of value as equals (ibid.).

European Union security co-ordination will involve high levels of pre-emption

The last point concluded that any exercise of political power to make collective choices of value should be publicly controlled by equally entitled citizens. That may well be a demanding standard. Yet it is arguable that there is an important limit to how far it is demanding of the CSDP. The exercise of power to make choices of value may not require that the democratic control of the CSDP be aggregated to a level any higher than the democratic systems of individual member states. In so far as political power is defined as a relationship where A can compel B to do something she would sooner not do, it is unclear how far CSDP involves an exercise of political power by the Union over its member states. All member states need to consent to all significant CSDP decisions, which cannot, in any case, be enforced on member states by Union law. Maybe, then, it is only when member states themselves come to coerce their own citizens in order to achieve what they have themselves agreed within the CSDP that the latter involves an exercise of political power that needs to be democratically controlled.

But does this argument rest on an adequate definition of political power? After all many concepts of power identify it with forms of constraint that fall well short of outright compulsion. Steven Lukes (2005) shows how power can be exercised just by structuring the availability of choices available to others. Michel Foucault argues that power even presupposes some measure of freedom to the extent it consists in attempts to influence the capacities of others to act (Hindess 1996). To consider whether CSDP might affect the action capacities of member states without at any point compelling them to act without their own consent, I want to focus on the particular problem of path-dependencies. Consider the use of CSDP to pool security capabilities; to invest in expensive joint defence projects; or to increase the 'inter-operability' of forces (Council of the European Union 2010). Some of these may be large decisions involving indivisibilities. There may, in other words, be limits to how far they can be broken down into small measures or into experiments that allow actors to discover pay-off structures, retreat and adjust to their environment if they get things wrong. To the contrary, commitments may need to be made to large investments years in advance. Yet, once initiated, collaborations may yield increasing returns. Capabilities may develop with use. Experience gained and skills developed in one mission will be available to subsequent ones. The individual components of any specialized division of labour in force structures or in arms procurement may have positive externalities for others.

Increasing returns will, however, create opportunity costs in 'switching paths' (Pierson 2000) once security co-ordinations are initiated. Indeed, exit options are likely to be limited in other ways. The more national forces are integrated into a specialized division of labour, the more difficult it may be even to attempt to revert to self-sufficiency in security provision: the more force structures may be based on the assumption that, if they are to be used at all, they are to be used with partners, and a specific and fixed group of partners. All that may, in turn, lock-in decisions about identity, institutions, economy and society, given the degree to which all those large questions are affected by ways in which polities organize their security, and with whom.

It may, therefore, be possible for security co-operation to develop through a succession of completely uncoerced decisions – to which each member state has willingly given its consent – and, yet, for the whole structure to be very much constraining of participating societies. Note, though, that the problem cannot be made to disappear by just abstaining from co-operation. *Non*-decisions may also lock-in forms of path-dependence. If some capabilities can only be jointly supplied through the collaboration of several partners over time, and if each act of co-operation involves some combination of high start-up costs and increasing returns, decisions *not* to co-operate will also constrain the means available to future choosers.

Decisions which lead to path-dependence do not so much re-allocate values as pre-empt the value choices that can be made by the democratically accountable representatives of future citizens. Path-dependence challenges the assumption that it is sufficient for actors to retain vetoes over decisions if they are to avoid others exercising power over them. In a process such as CSDP, path-dependence implies that member state governments at time t will constrain the choices available to the democratic majorities of their own member states at time $t + 1$, even where the latter are themselves veto holders. But that is not all. Assume that there are limits to how many co-operative initiatives can be pursued at any one time. After all, organizational theory emphasizes the limited capacities of institutions to mobilize attention and resources around more than a restricted number of priorities and a handful of shared definitions of the problem at hand (March and Olsen 1995). Assume further that those initiatives which do receive attention lock in particular paths, whilst some options which are neglected become cumulatively harder to pursue with time. If all this is true, all actors who have a role in deciding what is to be considered and how – including transnational groups of officials who work together in CSDP committees – will exercise power even over veto holders wherever they succeed in occupying limited space within the decision-making agenda or in establishing shared meanings and norms that frame the problem under consideration. They will limit options and frame problems before veto-holders get to exercise their vetoes. In sum, then, if all political power needs to be democratically controlled then that control may need to include decisions that pre-empt choice, as well as those that are coercively enforced.

European Union security co-ordination will require decisions about acceptable levels of risk

In addition to control over the political allocation of values, control over the basic shaping conditions of social life implies individuals should have control over the risks to which they are exposed (Beck 1992). At this point it might be objected that those taking part in European security missions are likely to be professional troops who have consented to a more risky way of life. Yet, it is unclear that responsibility for military personnel disappears where those forces are professional volunteers; and, in any case, military deployments amount to contingent liabilities affecting whole societies and not just professional forces. They expose societies to contingent risks that they may in the future have to commit more resources and more lives than anticipated; and to risks of retaliations.

In fact, European security co-operation may well involve two kinds of risk. Those involved in deploying multi-national forces; and those involved in encouraging specialization in the force structures of member states. Each decision to divide labours entails a gamble on the reliability of others: will partners really be there when they are needed? Yet, as already suggested, decisions *not* to divide labours may involve equally large gambles on self-sufficiency. In a dangerous world in which single member states may struggle to be self-sufficient security providers, risks in *not* co-operating may be as acute as those involved in co-operating.

A promoter of democratic peace must itself be able to demonstrate adequate public control of its own force deployments

A role in promoting democratic peace is, of course, not the only use to which European security co-operation might be put. Such an objective could even be dangerous and utopian in a world of plural values. Indeed, it would be indefensible and self-defeatingly non-Kantian if it involved treating others as means and not ends; as means towards a particular kind of peace desired by the European Union, and not as actors entitled to deliberate the conditions of their own peace and the conditions of their own self-government on a basis of equality (Jahn 2005).

But assume that European security co-operation could contribute to democratic peace without raising the last objection; that it could, in other words, be available to support others in *their own* democratic transitions. What would that presuppose for democratic control of security policy within the Union's own arena? To answer this question it helps to clarify the more credible claims of democratic peace theory. It plainly is not the case that democracies never go to war (Rosato 2003). Rather, democracies do not appear to go to war on democracies. Thus, the democratic peace amounts to a milieu goal. It involves persuading actors in other states that one reason why *they* might select democracy for *themselves* is that it would help contribute to an international public good in which the overall risk of conflict in the international system is likely to be reduced in proportion to the number of states that exercise democratic control over their own security policy. Indeed, the Union's own security strategy presents the link between democracy and security as just such a milieu goal: 'the quality of international society depends on the quality of governments that are its foundation. The best protection for our security is a world of well-governed democratic states' (Council of the European Union 2003: 10). If, however, the Union is to convince others that it is possible to co-ordinate on the achievement of such a milieu goal, it must avoid any impression that it may itself be depreciating the international public good characteristics of democratically controlled security. Thus, it must avoid any appearance of multi-lateralizing its own security in ways that could in practice reduce public control over force deployments by some of its own member states (Wagner 2006).

PARLIAMENTARY CONTROL?

The last section argued that European security co-ordination needs to be democratically controlled to the extent it involves legal obligations, rights, reallocations of value, risks, path-dependencies and attempts to promote democracy in the international system as a whole. In the remainder of the paper I assume that, taken together, these arguments presuppose democratic control of: (a) specific force deployments under CSDP; and of (b) decisions to use CSDP to cultivate particular capabilities rather than others.

Needless to say, my claim that democratic control over these two kinds of decision requires some element of parliamentary participation is by no means self-evident. To the contrary, I will show at various points in the remainder of the contribution that it needs to be made in the face of several forms of scepticism: as to the general utility and value of parliamentary control in contemporary democratic practice; as to the suitability of security policy to parliamentary control; and as to the ability of either national parliaments or the European Parliament (EP) to control Union decisions on behalf of voters.

Amongst arguments that question whether democratic control really requires parliamentary control, one has special relevance to this discussion: namely, the claim that parliaments have ceased to be important to modern forms of democratic control. According to that claim, voters can exercise adequate control through the choices they themselves make between political parties in elections (Klingemann *et al.* 1994: 241). The role of parliamentary politics has, accordingly, shrunk from one of exercising judgement over governments to one of sustaining the party disciplines needed for voters to exercise those judgements for themselves (Ranney 1954). In contrast to government in the shadow of electoral retribution, day-to-day accountability to parliaments often seems epiphenomenal to modern forms of democratic control. Even the 'forum role' that parliaments can exercise between elections is, arguably, being eroded by modern media, which are more compelling, more watched, more demanding and more independent in forcing governments to justify their decisions than executive-dominated parliaments could ever be.

The possibility that mass media and mass party systems might allow voters direct control over *executive* branches of government in ways that can 'bracket' out parliaments, deserves much more attention than it has received either in discussions of the democratic control of security or of EU decisions. On the one hand, it seems to anticipate the argument that security is properly a matter for executive discretion (see for example Thomas Jefferson, quoted in Corwin [1917: 203]). The objection that security decisions need to be taken speedily and without betraying information that could be valuable to the intended targets of any military action or dissuasion works more persuasively against *ex ante* procedures of parliamentary authorization than *ex post* judgements by voters. On the other hand the standard democratic deficit argument that European integration empowers executives at the expense of parliaments is less persuasive if voters can, indeed, exercise direct control over executives through the choices they make at the ballot box.

Whether it really is possible to manage without some element of parliamentary participation depends on what institutional means are needed to realize minimum democratic standards of: (1) public control; with (2) political equality; and (3) individual rights to justification (Forst 2007). Whilst others have demonstrated why the first two elements form part of what Bohman calls a 'democratic minimum' (Bohman 2007; see also Weale 1999), the need for the third requires a bit more explanation. Since liberal democratic systems are committed to regarding individuals as 'morally autonomous persons' they are also committed to only coercing them in ways those individuals can themselves accept as good or right (Rawls 1993: 38). Note that this duty is owed to each individual, as it follows from the original justification for democracy itself by ideals of personal autonomy. Thus, even majorities elected on a basis of political equality to exercise powers of public control owe each individual whose views have otherwise been set aside a justification that collectively binding decisions have, indeed, been made in ways that oblige those individuals (Habermas 1996: 67).

I labour the point about justification, since in many ways the value added of parliamentary politics lies in the distinctive and mutually reinforcing ways in which it can link justification on the one hand with public control and political equality on the other. Parliaments do not just provide continuous public control between elections or proceduralize political equality by the simple means of electing representatives elected on the principle 'one person, one vote'. They also provide a setting in which representatives elected on a basis of political equality, specialized for public debate, incentivized by political competition and backed by controlling powers can insist on justifications, weight and sift them, and reward and sanction them. Whereas elements of public control with political equality can indeed be delivered by the abstract systems of mass electoral democracy that allow citizens some scope to control governments directly through the ballot box, parliamentary politics completes the link to the in-depth weighing of justifications. Two quotations capture the point.

> Justified and binding decisions about policies and laws demand, on the one hand, that deliberation and decision-making take place face to face. On the other hand, at the level of simple and direct interactions, not all citizens can join in the shared exercise of such a practice. A solution to this problem is provided by the *parliamentary principle* of establishing representative bodies for deliberation and decision-making. (Habermas 1996: 170; emphasis original)

> Representative bodies are often taunted by their enemies as being places of mere talk and *bavardage*. There has seldom been more misplaced derision. I know not how a representative body can more usefully employ itself than in talk ... The Parliament has an office to be a Congress of Opinions; an arena in which every opinion can produce itself in full light to be tested in adverse controversy ... where those whose opinion is overruled can feel that it is set aside not by a mere act of will but for reasons that commend themselves to representatives of a majority. (Mill 1972: 239–40)

Crucial here is that the exchange of justifications in a parliamentary setting can be made to operate over issues and over time. Over issues, parliaments can in principle test any one justification in relation to another across the whole range of matters for which a polity is responsible. This is important, since public control of single decisions taken in sequence would fail to encompass value trade-offs between issues, negative externalities or even cumulative unintended consequences. Over time, parliamentary debate puts the justification for decisions 'on the record'. That, in turn, contributes to 'losers' consent'. By requiring 'winners' to justify decisions, it establishes what arguments may need to be countered if the decision is to be reversed. Where, indeed, decisions are regarded as 'temporary closure devices' within a search for wider understanding and agreement (Eriksen 2009: 47–53), parliamentary debate records successive iterations in processes of public justification.

WHICH PARLIAMENTARISM?

Thus far, the paper has used democratic theory to identify what it is about the CSDP that may require its democratic control. It has further argued that democratic control requires some measure of parliamentary participation, particularly in linking basic standards of public control with political equality to the justifications of decisions. However, as Immanuel Kant (1933: 637) famously put it, 'ought' implies 'can'; or at least it does so if our aim is to avoid utopianism (Weale 1999: 8–9). Any discussion of feasibility has to start out from a frank acknowledgement of constraints on parliamentary control at both the national and European levels.

The notion that Union decisions can be adequately controlled by national parliaments is open to at least the following objections. First, national parliaments only have individual control over Council members and not collective control over the Council. Second, there are limits to how far one political system can be controlled through the democratic institutions of another (Lord 2004: 181–2). For example, the costs to national parliaments of acquiring the specialized forms of expertise needed for effective democratic control will increase where they have to monitor both domestic and Union matters. This is no small matter. The influence of contemporary legislatures depends on their ability to overcome asymmetries of information (Krehbiel 1991) and expertise that typically put them at a disadvantage to executive actors. Third, national parliaments are structurally unequal both in their powers over security policies and in their general powers over their governments, which are, in turn, unequal in their weight in the Union's political system.

The last point is worth elaborating in relation to public control over troop deployments. Of the national parliaments included in Wolfgang Wagner's study of powers over troop deployments, seven are classified as having a high level of control over military deployments (Denmark, Finland, Germany, Ireland, Slovakia, Spain and Sweden); five as having a medium level of control (Austria, the Czech Republic, Italy, Luxembourg and the Netherlands) and seven as having a low level of control (Belgium, France, Greece, Hungary, Poland, Portugal and the United Kingdom) (Wagner 2006: 11). This classification, however, is based only on an analysis of procedures for mandating military deployments. How powerful any national parliament is likely to be in exercising those procedures is also likely to be affected by its overall strength within its political system. Thus, it is useful to add more general classifications of the relative power of national parliaments to Wagner's undoubtedly helpful typology. Paul Pennings (2000) has devised a ranking based on the relative formal powers of governments and parliaments to dismiss or dissolve the other. Döring et al. (1995) have produced a ranking based more on the power of governments to dominate the parliaments through party systems, agenda controls and limits to the resources available to parliaments. These two rankings suggest two qualifications to Wagner's classification. On the Döring *et al.* (though not on the Pennings) ranking Germany needs to be reclassified as only a 'balanced' system and not one in which 'parliament dominates government'. On both rankings the Spanish system needs to be reclassified as one where 'government dominates parliament'. This confirms that national parliaments are, indeed, unequal in their controlling powers over their own governments. But it also has a further implication: several feasible coalitions for deploying force under CSDP can be put together without involving any member state whose national parliament assuredly enjoys high levels of control over military deployments.

Is there scope, however, to compensate for unevenness in the powers of national parliament by involving the European Parliament, which is, after all, the one parliament whose powers and practices are common to the Union as a whole? Through cunning as much as design (Bono 2006), the EP has acquired a role in relation to the CSDP which demonstrates that horizontal checks on the Council as a whole can indeed complement any vertical checks national parliaments exercise on its individual members. Inter-institutional agreements now allow for the disclosure of sensitive security information to a special committee of five Members of the European Parliament (MEPs), and for 'joint consultation' meetings which cover both implementation and budgetary implications (Barbé and Herranz Surraillés 2008: 81). Whilst, perhaps unsurprisingly, the Council has not conceded the EP's 'maximalist' demand that CSDP missions should be approved by an absolute majority of MEPs, the EP has on occasions unilaterally passed resolutions stating the terms on which it would have approved CSDP missions had it the formal power to do so (ibid.). This could develop into a source of influence in the future in so far as governments conclude that it is better to discuss the terms of missions with the Parliament than leave themselves exposed, if things subsequently go wrong, to the charge that they did not take all risks into account at the time of deployment. Such a trend could also be encouraged if the present practice is continued of co-financing security missions out of the Commission's budget, which, of course, has to be co-decided with the EP (Monar 1997; Thym 2006:113–17).

Yet, there are well-known questions about how well the exercise of any of the Parliament's powers is linked to the voters in a manner sufficient to ensure public control. To the extent European elections are second-order (Reif and Schmitt 1980), they do not structure voter choice around a form of political competition relevant to the Union itself. They produce little debate about the views that should be represented in a coming European Parliament, and little assessment of the views represented in an outgoing European Parliament. As such, it is unclear how far they assure public control either *ex ante* or *ex post*.

If, however, there are likely to be shortcomings in either national or European Parliament monitoring of the CSDP, could those shortcomings be anticipated in arrangements for the co-ordination and distribution of parliamentary functions across the two levels? Multi-level solutions should after all be available within a multi-level system of governance (Scharpf 2009). Still, we need to tread carefully. Whilst COSAC (The Conference of European Affairs Committees of Parliaments of the European Union) surveys of national parliaments and the EP indicate wide support for 'interparliamentary scrutiny', they also demonstrate disagreement on how that might be attempted. The European Parliament's response to one survey called for 'a new and innovative form of interparliamentary committee' involving representatives of national parliaments and its own committees on foreign affairs, and defence and security. Indeed, the EP proposed that it should organize the 'meetings and the premises', in order to avoid any need for a 'new form of administrative structure'. In contrast, five national parliaments argued that the involvement of the EP should be limited to the exchange of information. Any 'forum' established to aid co-ordination should be 'composed of members of national parliaments only'. The five parliaments more or less agreed with the Finnish *Eduskunta* that 'any EP involvement would be hard to reconcile with the Lisbon Treaty' which 'precludes any arrangement where the European Parliament could influence the conclusions of intergovernmental co-operation' (COSAC 2010: 17–27).

Behind this spat lies a deeper structural problem that needs to be identified and navigated if the feasibility of using multi-level solutions to improve the parliamentary control of the CSDP is to be demonstrated. Although fashionable, it is by no means self-evident that co-ordination by national parliaments and the EP on CSDP matters will yield superior parliamentary control. Consider an argument from the wider democratic deficit debate which runs as follows: whilst there are many familiar reasons for believing that it is hard to institutionalize democratic control of the European arena (Scharpf 1999), there is one approach to democratic control to which the Union is conceivably better suited than most of the political systems of its member states. Precisely because it is not an integrated polity, its decisions are often exposed to a remarkably high number of veto points (Mény 2002). CSDP decisions – whether they are decisions to deploy troops or to co-ordinate the development of military capabilities – require unanimity of participating governments. Each of the latter is, in turn, constrained in different ways by their own parties and coalition relationships between parties, by non-coincident electoral cycles, by non-identical procedures for authorizing force deployments and so on. On top of all that the EP, as seen, may exercise some horizontal scrutiny.

A particular advantage of multiple veto points is that they can work even under relatively unfavourable conditions to reduce the risk of arbitrary and unjustified decisions. Assume a high level of executive domination of parliaments across most member states that is, none the less, neither complete, nor unconditional nor constant. Under such conditions, parliamentary scrutiny of CSDP decisions on deployments or on the cultivation of military capabilities could function like a Condorcet jury. Even if the chances of any one national parliament acting with sufficient autonomy to expose weaknesses in justifications for CSDP are only fractionally higher than evens, the chances that they will collectively identify those weaknesses will increase with the number of parliaments which have to be convinced of the case for a decision (See Goodin's [2003] discussion of 'democracy as a condorcet truth-tracker'.) The advantage of requiring CSDP decisions to run the gauntlet of scrutiny by several parliaments could be further increased by the benefits of including some margin of uncertainty in arrangements for accountability. Decision-makers are more likely to anticipate from the outset how their decisions can on balance be justified against all possible lines of criticism where they do not have too much advance information on how exactly those decisions are likely to be challenged and by whom (Chambers 2004: 390–1). Thus, it might be a mistake for inter-parliamentary co-ordination to take a form that substitutes for the individual judgement of different parliaments on the wisdom of CSDP initiatives: that reduces the multiplicity of veto points; that narrows the uncertainties and diversity of challenges faced by those who are required to justify the CSDP; that attempts to co-opt parliaments to a received view of CSDP; and so on.

If these, though, are possible pitfalls of co-ordination, what might be the costs and risks of *not* co-ordinating national and European parliamentary scrutiny of the CSDP? One difficulty follows from the very flexibility of CSDP. Both security missions and co-ordinations on the development of security capabilities need be only to some degree coalitions of the willing. Thus, in the absence of co-ordination on rigorous standards of scrutiny, country participation in security missions could conceivably be affected by differences in the pliability of individual national parliaments.

A converse difficulty is that even powerful domestic institutions in powerful member states sometimes appear constrained in how far they feel it is prudent to criticize security co-operation (see especially Wagner 2006: 32). Factors that might deter national parliaments from unilateral opposition plausibly include concerns about: (a) the overall credibility of defence co-operation; (b) the reputation of their own country as a reliable security partner; (c) patterns of reciprocity; and (d) the bargaining costs of re-opening agreements to co-operate which have been negotiated with difficulty (see also Thym 2006: 122). Yet, in so far as parliaments may feel individually constrained from criticizing CSDP decisions which some of them might have questioned jointly, unco-ordinated scrutiny will involve an element of prisoners' dilemma. Greater information about one another's intentions could ease at least some of the foregoing constraints on unilateral opposition.

If, then, co-ordination has the dangers and benefits I have suggested, and if national parliaments and the European Parliament have the weaknesses and strengths I have depicted, can we at last identify some distribution of parliamentary functions across the national and European levels that might improve on existing arrangements? Here it is useful to return to the argument that security is unsuited to parliamentary control. That argument ignores the variety of forms that parliamentary control can take and the degree to which they can be adapted to any need for speed and secrecy in security decisions. For example, *ex ante* and *ex post* controls can be combined in different ways. Representative bodies can explore with governments the conditions under which force might be used ahead of time. Greater reliance on deliberation before the event, rather than sanction after the event may, in any case, have intrinsic merits (Mansbridge 2004). In complex systems where cause–effect relationships may be elusive, and decisions may involve too many hands for responsibility for actions always to be attributable, it may make more sense to base accountability on a logic of appropriateness rather than a logic of consequence: to ask whether all actors followed agreed norms, rather than to attempt the difficult task of unpicking precisely whose behaviour led to some undesired consequence (March and Olsen 1995). Moreover, actors may themselves find it easier to act where they are supplied with some advance guidance on which decisions are likely to be justifiable and which not.

Note, too, that the one obvious source of *ex ante* control over force deployments concerns precisely the other kind of decision I have suggested should be the subject of parliamentary scrutiny: namely, decisions about the cultivation of capabilities. Not only might it seem obvious that both kinds of decision should be 'programmed' by similar values in dialogue with bodies capable of legitimating choices of value. But, of course, decisions about capabilities constrain decisions about deployments *ex ante*.

Of course, *ex ante* accountability will often provide an incomplete guide for how decisions should be made in emergencies. Indeed, the very phenomenon of executive prerogative to which parliamentary control of security deployments is opposed has its roots in John Locke's observation that it is not only likely that public dangers will arise that are unanticipated by existing laws; but, worse than that, it is at least imaginable that widely held conceptions of the public good may at some point require governments to break the law. As it happens Locke's (1977: 199–204) own solution was laughably unsatisfactory (we should trust in heaven to judge whether those who rule us have used their discretion wisely under such circumstances). Yet, solutions to the problem he identified are suggested by four centuries of subsequent experience in designing institutions for the constraint of the arbitrary use of power. The United States War Powers Act illustrates the possibility of allowing governments time-limited exercises of discretion in the deployment of force before they have to justify those deployments to a representative body, or even seek formal authorization for them.

Now in the European context, authorizations for force deployments – and probably most decisions about the development of capabilities – would almost certainly have to be in the hands of national parliaments. As long as political community is limited at the European level there are likely to be limits to how far European security missions can be legitimated as such, especially where they involve high risks of casualties. It is perhaps equally obvious that, as long as military establishments remain national in nature, only national parliaments will be able to satisfy basic institutional requirements for public responsibility: only they will be able to sanction mistakes by demanding accounts from those with political responsibility for decisions and for resources; by forcing resignations; by threatening budget lines; and so on.

Yet, as seen, the development of expertise needed to overcome asymmetries of information is crucial to the capacity of representative bodies to control executive decisions. Here national parliaments face the difficulty that knowledge and expertise of the issues to be monitored in European security co-ordination are to some degree specific to the European arena. Even the Common Foreign and Security Policy (CFSP) and CSDP have their own technical instruments, governance committees and histories. Their informed scrutiny may even require knowledge of the range of the Union's policies. After all, decisions to mediate security co-operation through the EU in the first place may be partly motivated by holistic concepts of security in which security problems are seen as requiring simultaneous solutions in economic, social, governance, judicial and ecological dimensions. Thus, a proper understanding of CSDP decisions may also require understanding of how they are co-ordinated with many other Union policies (Smith 1996). Now, networks of national parliaments could conceivably accumulate such expertise without much help from the EP by, for example, sharing information and assessments, as executive actors themselves do (Bicchi and Carta 2010). Still, at the end of the day, national parliaments face opportunity costs in developing expertise on Union matters: time spent on detailed monitoring of Union policies is time not spent on domestic politics

Whilst, then, it would make sense for national parliaments to control decisions their own member states make about CSDP deployments and capabilities, it also makes sense to involve the EP in the scrutiny of justifications for those decisions. Such a division of labour could offset weaknesses in parliamentary control at the two levels. Authorization of deployments and decisions to develop capabilities would be in the hands of parliaments that are publicly controlled by first-order elections. Scrutiny of justifications for both kinds of decision would be shared with the EP with its advantages over national parliaments in overcoming asymmetries of information and linking powers horizontally across Union policies. Not only does that seem feasible. Some of it could even be achieved by parliaments at the two levels adapting their own internal procedures to make better and more co-ordinated use of existing powers.

Note, though, that any co-ordinated scrutiny would ideally combine the positive externalities of dividing labours and exchanging views with a strong norm that it is for each parliament to make its own judgement on CSDP decisions. As seen, the parliaments of the Union need to co-ordinate their control of the CSDP just enough to overcome prisoners' dilemmas that might otherwise inhibit their individual opposition to decisions. Yet they also need to avoid co-ordinating in ways which might remove the advantages of requiring justifications to pass muster with several parliaments that are prepared to test them critically.

CONCLUSION

On the assumption that in liberal democracies there can be no legitimacy without democracy and there can be no democracy without representation,

I have attempted to identify what considerations of democratic theory would require the democratic and parliamentary control of the CSDP. On the further assumption that 'ought implies can', I have also asked whether the normative case for the democratic and parliamentary control of the CSDP stands up to practical constraints, including general shortcomings in parliamentary politics, difficulties in securing public control of the Union through the European Parliament or national parliaments, and problems of parliamentary participation in security decisions. I have tried to answer the question of feasibility by suggesting ways in which both national parliaments and the European Parliament might be involved in both the control of CSDP decisions and scrutiny of justifications that are offered for them. Yet, I have tended to suggest that national parliaments should undertake rather more of the control and the EP should concern itself rather more with the scrutiny of justifications. Some may see that as confining the EP to a lesser role. I do not. The weighing and sifting of justifications is the value added of parliamentary politics.

Biographical note: Christopher Lord is Professor at ARENA – Centre for European Studies, University of Oslo, Norway.

REFERENCES

Barbé, E. and Herranz Surralles, A. (2008) 'The power and practice of the European Parliament in security policies', in D. Peters, W. Wagner and N. Deitelhoff (eds), *The Parliamentary Control of European Security Policy*, RECON Report No 6, Oslo: ARENA, pp. 77–108.

Beck, U. (1992) *Risk Society: Towards a New Modernity*, London: Sage.

Bicchi, F. and Carta, C. (2010) 'The COREU/CORTESY network and the circulation of information within EU foreign policy', *RECON Online Working Paper 2010/01*, Oslo: ARENA.

Bohman, J. (2007) 'Democratising the transnational polity: the European Union and the presuppositions of democracy', in E.O. Eriksen (ed.), *How to Reconstitute Democracy in Europe? Proceedings from the RECON Opening Conference*, RECON Report No 3, Oslo: ARENA, pp. 65–90.

Bono, G. (2006) 'Challenges of democratic oversight of EU security policies', *European Security* 15(4): 431–49.

Buchanan, J. and Tullock, G. (1962) *The Calculus of Consent. Logical Foundations of Constitutional Democracy*, Ann Arbor, MI: University of Michigan Press.

Chambers, S. (2004) 'Behind closed doors: publicity, secrecy, and the quality of deliberation', *The Journal of Political Philosophy* 17(4): 389–410.

Cohen, M., March, J. and Olsen, J. (1972) 'A garbage can model of administrative choice', *Administrative Science Quarterly* 17(1): 1–25.

Corwin, E. (1917) *The President's Control of Foreign Relations*, Princeton, NJ: Princeton University Press.

COSAC (2010) *Fourteenth Bi-annual Report. Developments in European Union Procedures and Practices Relevant to Parliamentary Scrutiny*, Brussels: COSAC.

Council of the European Union (2003) *A Secure Europe in a Better World. European Security Strategy*, Brussels: Council of Ministers.
Council of the European Union (2010) 'Council conclusions on military capability development: 3055th Foreign Affairs (defence) Council Meeting', Council of Ministers, Brussels, 9 December.
Döring, H. (ed.) (1995) *Parliaments and Majority Rule in Western Europe*, Frankfurt am Main: Campus Verlag.
Duchêne, F. (1972) 'Europe's role in world peace', in R. Mayne (ed.), *Europe Tomorrow. Sixteen Europeans Look Ahead*, London: Collins, pp. 32–47.
Eriksen, E.O. (2009) *The Unfinished Democratization of Europe*, Oxford: Oxford University Press.
Forst, R. (2007) *Das Recht auf Rechtfertigung. Elemente einer Konstruktivistischen Theorie der Gerechtigkeit*, Frankfurt am Main: Suhrkamp.
Goodin, R. (2003) *Reflective Democracy*, Oxford: Oxford University Press.
Habermas, J. (1996) *Between Facts and Norms. Contributions to a Discourse Theory of Law*, Cambridge, MA: Polity Press.
Hill, C. (2003) *The Changing Politics of Foreign Policy*, Basingstoke: Palgrave.
Hindess, B. (1996) *Discourses of Power from Hobbes to Foucault*, Oxford: Blackwell.
Jahn, B. (2005) 'Kant, Mill and illiberal legacies in international affairs', *International Organisation* 59(1): 177–207.
Kant, I. (1933) [1787] *Critique of Pure Reason*, London: Macmillan.
Klingemann, H.D., Hofferbert, R. and Budge, I. (1994) *Parties, Policies and Democracy*, Boulder, CO: Westview.
Krehbiel, K. (1991) *Information and Legislative Organisation*, Ann Arbor, MI: University of Michigan Press.
Locke, J. (1977) [1690] *Two Treatises of Government*, London: Everyman.
Lord, C. (2004) *A Democratic Audit of the European Union*, Basingstoke: Palgrave Macmillan.
Lukes, S. (2005) [1974] *Power a Radical View*, Basingstoke: Palgrave Macmillan.
Manners, I. (2002) 'Normative power Europe: a contradiction in terms?', *Journal of Common Market Studies* 40(2): 235–58.
Mansbridge, J. (2004) 'Representation revisited. Introduction to the case against electoral accountability', *Democracy and Society* 2(1): 12–13.
March, J. and Olsen, J. (1995) *Democratic Governance*, New York: Free Press.
Mény, Y. (2002) 'De la Démocratie en Europe: old concepts, new challenges', *Journal of Common Market Studies* 41(1): 1–13.
Mill, J.S. (1972) [1861] *Utilitarianism. On Liberty and Considerations on Representative Government*, London: Dent.
Monar, J. (1997) 'The finances of the Union's intergovernmental pillars', *Journal of Common Market Studies* 35(1): 57–78.
Pennings, P. (2000) 'Parliamentary control of the executive in 47 democracies', Paper presented to ECPR Joint Sessions, April.
Pettit, P. (1997) *Republicanism. A Theory of Freedom and Government*, Oxford: Oxford University Press.
Pierson, P. (2000) 'Increasing returns, path dependence and the study of politics', *American Political Science Review* 94(2): 251–67.
Ranney, A. (1954) *The Doctrine of Party Responsible Government. Its Origins and Present State*, Urbana, IL: University of Illinois Press.
Rawls, J. (1993) *Political Liberalism*, New York: Columbia University Press.
Reif, K.-H. and Schmitt, H. (1980) 'Nine second-order national elections: a conceptual framework for the analysis of European election results', *European Journal of Political Research* 8(1): 3–45.

Rosato, S. (2003) 'The flawed logic of democratic peace theory', *American Political Science Review* 97(4): 585–602.

Scharpf, F. (1999) *Governing in Europe. Effective and Democratic*, Oxford: Oxford University Press.

Scharpf, F. (2009) 'Legitimacy in the multilevel European polity', *European Political Science Review* 1(2): 173–204.

Smith, M. (1996) 'The EU as an international actor', in J. Richardson (ed.), *European Union, Power and Policy-Making*, 1st edn, London: Routledge.

Thym, D. (2006) 'Beyond Parliament's reach: the role of the European Parliament in the CFSP', *European Foreign Affairs Review* 11(1): 109–27.

Waever, O. (1996) 'European security identitites', *Journal of Common Market Studies* 34(1): 103–32.

Wagner, W. (2006) 'Parliamentary control of military missions: accounting for pluralism', *Occasional Paper 12*, Geneva: Geneva Centre for the Democratic Control of Armed Forces (DCAF).

Weale, A. (1999) *Democracy*, Palgrave: Basingstoke.

A contradiction in terms? NGOs, democracy, and European foreign and security policy

Jutta Joachim and Matthias Dembinski

ABSTRACT   In this contribution, we use a governance lens to assess the possibilities for political participation of non-governmental organizations (NGOs) in the European Common Foreign and Security Policy (CFSP). We illustrate their engagement in the case of the European Code of Conduct/Common Position on Arms Export. We show that, while processes related to the emergence of the Code fit the description of intergovernmental approaches, developments since then, however, more closely resemble governance. With the growing institutionalization of the CFSP in general, and that related to the Code in particular, access points for NGOs became increasingly available. Through information and symbolic politics as well as rhetorical entrapment, civil society organizations contributed not only to the tightening and widening of the Code's provisions, but also to the increasing willingness of governments to provide information to each other as well as their own publics about arms exports.

INTRODUCTION

A deep rift cleaves academic work on the European Union (EU). While research related to the former first pillar has been profiting from the incorporation of governance approaches, research into the foreign and security policy is still dominated by state-centric perspectives. Although there have been some attempts to introduce governance to the second pillar in recent years (see, for example, Webber *et al.* 2004), they were inspired by a broad understanding of governance and focused, for the most part, on the Commission (e.g., Kirchner 2006), the Council bureaucracy (Vanhoonacker *et al.* 2010) or on networks between state representatives and EU bodies (Mérand *et al.* 2010). In contrast to research on the first pillar, interest and civil society groups have thus far received little attention in studies of the European Common Foreign and Security Policy (CFSP).[1]

In this contribution we help to fill this gap in the literature. We assess the role of non-governmental organizations (NGOs) in the formulation of EU foreign policy and their relationships with EU institutions. Ongoing changes in the second pillar, including the establishment of new institutions, the broadening of security, and growing interdependencies between states indicate that the opportunities for these organizations to become involved in the CFSP may have increased. Drawing on a governance perspective, which emphasizes political processes and conceives of them as more open and subject to wider participation than in the intergovernmental approach, with state and non-state actors co-operating and contributing through their knowledge and resources to particular outcomes, we study the adoption of the European Code of Conduct on Arms Exports in May of 1998 and subsequent developments (Council of the European Union 1998). This represents a 'hard case' for NGO participation.

Weapons production and sales belong to the most sensitive area of state sovereignty: defence. Hence, we would expect governments to seek not only the maintenance of their autonomy and flexibility in this area, but also to minimize public involvement. While we do find some support for this assumption, particularly in the early 1990s, later developments confound the image of an entirely state-controlled process. We show, first, that NGOs mattered and benefitted from ongoing institutionalization in the second pillar. They played an important role during both the agenda-setting and the implementation phases of the Code of Conduct regarding weapons exports. Prior to its adoption, they provided policy blueprints and, together with the Commission and the European Parliament (EP), exerted pressure on governments. Once in place, NGOs used the Code to instigate beauty contests by singling out governments with good and best weapons export practices and shaming those that violated the principles agreed upon at the European level. Second, we also provide evidence that NGOs had an impact. Although weapons sales have not yet declined significantly, NGOs have used the Code to change the rules of the game through which they are approved. Over time governments became increasingly willing to provide more information to each other as well as their own publics about arms exports. Moreover, following the effective lobbying by transnational coalitions and the exploitation of growing interdependencies between the national and European levels, NGOs contributed to more restrictive arms controls regimes in individual member states that were reflective of the European Code of Conduct, as we illustrate in the case of Spain. Finally, despite initial opposition, EU member states adopted a Common Position in December of 2008, which turned the Code that had been intended as a non-committal arrangement into a legally binding framework (Council of the European Union 2008). While we are cognisant of the important role that the defence industry plays with respect to weapons procurement, we limit our focus exclusively to NGOs since corporate involvement has already been documented elsewhere (e.g., Schmitt 2000).

The paper is divided into three parts. Drawing on the governance literature on civil society and interest groups in the EU, we first describe NGO engagement within the CFSP more generally and identify several factors that facilitate their involvement: Europeanization; access points; and norms. We then turn to the Code of Conduct on Arms Exports in the second section, which is divided into two parts: emergence and further development. While NGOs have contributed to both, they noticeably gained influence once the EU-wide regime regarding weapons sales was in place. In the concluding section we discuss implications for the conception of CFSP. The data in this contribution stems from: (1) EU, NGO and governmental documents; (2) interviews we conducted with EU officials, representatives of NGOs and governments; and (3) news and scholarly articles.

FROM INTERGOVERNMENTALISM TO GOVERNANCE

Governance approaches have been widely employed in studying the first and third pillars, but they have been virtually absent from studies related to the CFSP. Because the conduct of foreign and security policy seemed to follow its own integration logic, state-centric explanations dominated. While the CFSP still exhibits unique aspects, it is no longer as 'distinct from other EU policy areas [as] before' (Vanhoonacker *et al.* 2010: 3).

Given these changes, a governance perspective is appealing because it draws attention to 'institutions, corporate interests, civil society, and transnational organizations' (Pierre 2000: 4; see also Kohler-Koch and Rittberger 2006) and how they become involved in policy-making (Krahmann 2003; Webber *et al.* 2004: 5). From a governance point of view, non-state actors contribute to the development of new rules and norms at the European level and function as transmission belts, transporting information back to the domestic level where it can be used by societal groups to formulate legitimate demands upon their governments. Several related factors are frequently mentioned that encourage their inclusion at the supranational level: Europeanization; the availability of access points; and norms.

Europeanization, defined as process by which domestic policy areas are becoming increasingly subject to European policy-making (Börzel and Risse 2003), creates incentives for civil society organizations to direct their attention towards Brussels (Featherstone 2003: 7) and 'opportunities for political action, which actors and groups will seek to exploit' (Stone Sweet and Sandholtz 1997: 305). While this pattern of 'co-evolution' (Eichener and Voelzkow 1994; Kohler-Koch 1996) has been aptly demonstrated in first pillar cases (e.g., Greenwood 2003), it also seems to fit developments in the second pillar. As one NGO activist observed: 'The Europeanization process has created new opportunities for civil society and parliaments to hold their governments accountable' (Bauer and Bromley 2004a: 144).

Following the formal establishment of the CFSP with the Maastricht Treaty in 1993 and propelled by the changing notion of what 'security' means, established NGOs began to mobilize around foreign and security policy issues at the EU level. They established platforms or networks to multiply their strength (Dembinski 2009: 159), such as the Network for Civil Peace Services (EN.CPS), and the European Platform for Conflict Prevention and Transformation and the International Action Network on Small Arms (IANSA).

In 2001 the European Peacebuilding Liaison Office (EPLO) was founded and was recognized by the Commission in 2010 as a major NGO network in the field of peacebuilding (Interview 4, 2011). While some of these networks and organizations are rooted in social movements and grass-roots organizations at the national level, others, such as the International Security Information Service, Europe (ISIS-Europe) or the International Crisis Group, both of which were founded in 1995, are more akin to think-tanks. They place almost exclusive emphasis on the generation of expertise in lieu of building a large constituency. Despite, or perhaps because of, these differences, there are, according to one observer, 'significant links between the organizations, with a division of labour and subject expertise, sharing of information and a significant degree of personnel exchange over the years' (Stavrianakis 2010: 7).

Europeanization and co-evolution also influence the strategies employed by civil society and interest groups. According to Justin Greenwood (2009), NGOs adjust to the technocratic culture and style of the EU. They place great emphasis on lobbying based on well-researched information and tend to refrain from more overt protest and highly symbolic actions. This description also seems to apply to NGOs working on foreign and security policy issues at the European level. Most of the Brussels-based NGOs have embarked on a professional advocacy style that stresses the provision of information, consultation, and networking with like-minded actors inside the institutions. In addition to shaping the strategies that NGOs employ and sparking the establishment of new networks and organizations, Europeanization can also empower NGOs more indirectly, owing to the establishment of new institutions, which may create new access points for NGOs.

While the CFSP has generally been characterized as a rather inaccessible policy system, this description no longer fits political realities. As growing interdependencies and new security issues replace the agenda of classical diplomacy and the success of foreign policy initiatives hinges on both their public involvement and acceptance, working with NGOs and civil society actors has become almost mandatory. Reports from observers of the CFSP confirm this, suggesting an increasing willingness of state representatives and Council bureaucrats to interact with NGOs in the field of security.

While initially sporadic, informal and ad hoc (Gourlay 2006: 19), these exchanges are showing signs of institutionalization as evidenced, for example, by the adoption of Recommendations for Enhancing Co-operation with NGOs in the Framework of EU Civilian Crisis Management by the Political and Security Committee in November 2006 (Dembinski 2009: 159). Changes are particularly striking within the Working Party of Conventional Arms Exports (COARM), where it has become common procedure for the national diplomats to meet with NGOs on the first day of their regular two-day fall meeting (Interviews 2 and 6, 2011).

In addition to the Council, the European Parliament constitutes an important access point for NGOs on foreign and security policy matters. They maintain particularly close relations to its Committee on Foreign Affairs. When asked about the reasons for this contact, one of our interview partners answered thus:

> It is useful to engage the European Parliament on foreign policy issues. We see them as an ally, and we are an ally to them. ... We even work well with

conservatives, because MEPs care about parliamentary control and oversight. We are on the same side of the debate, and generally the European Parliament is easier to get to because MEPs are representatives and they get paid to talk to us. (Interview 4, 2011)

Members of the European Parliament (MEPs) regularly attend dialogue meetings organized by NGOs and rely on them for expertise. As one MEP put it: 'The information provided by NGOs is critical. Organizations, such as Amnesty International, Oxfam, or Saferworld, prepare very good and solid reports to which hardly anyone can object' (Interview 9, 2011).

As the Commission has moved from being an observer to an active participant in the CFSP, enjoying *de facto* agenda-setting power in areas of mixed competences and being in charge of implementing programmes, it has also become an important access point for, and promoter of, NGO activities. Its relevance for NGOs varies, however, across issues. It appears to be more pronounced with respect to so-called cross-pillar issues, like conflict prevention and peace-building, which lie at the nexus of security and development (Sicurelli 2008). Close ties exist between the Commission and concerned NGOs. Already in 1997, for example, the Commission kick-started and funded the Conflict Prevention Network (Rummel 2003) followed by a one-year pilot project, the Conflict Prevention Partnership in 2005. Furthermore, in 2007, the Commission initiated and supported the NGO 'Initiative for Peacebuilding' and, in July 2010, its successor, the Civil Society Dialogue Network (CSDN). Designed to facilitate dialogue on peace-building issues between civil society and EU institutions, the network is managed by EPLO (European Peacebuilding Liaison Office 2011). More importantly, the Commission has been using funds from the Instrument for Stability (IfS) to finance the Peace-building Partnership, launched in 2007, with a view to strengthening the capacity of respective NGOs and their institutional links with EU offices (Bayne and Trolliet 2009).

Finally, scholars have found *institutional norms* to be conducive to NGO engagement. According to two leading scholars, they provide the basis for 'moral leverage' (Keck and Sikkink 1998: 23). Civil society organizations can exert pressure on policy-makers by reminding them of their normative commitments and by drawing attention to the discrepancies between these and their actions.

Norms, Europeanization and the availability of new access points have been conducive factors for NGOs to become involved in the regulation of arms exports and to challenge the unchallenged control that governments previously had in the policy domain.

EMPIRICAL OBSERVATIONS

The political process leading up to the binding Code of Conduct on Arms Exports in 2008 can be divided into two phases: (1) from the Luxembourg Council meeting in 1991 to the adoption of the Code in 1998, and (2) from then to its legalization in 2008. During both periods NGOs played an active role. Relying primarily on insider strategies, they offered the blueprint for the EU-wide system on arms control, provided reasons why it was needed, and mounted pressure for states to support it. Furthermore, NGOs used what had been intended as a rather loose and non-committal framework to entrap governments and deprive them of complete control regarding the use of information concerning armament sales. Nevertheless, during the two aforementioned phases, their impact was more limited during the first and increased over the course of the second. We argue that these initial obstacles were the result of restricted access points, the lack of a clear EU standard of good conduct, and the NGOs' own difficulties in mobilizing their resources.

From the Luxembourg criteria to the adoption of the Code of Conduct on Arms Exports

In 1991 the EU members established the ad hoc COARM working group with a view to harmonizing national arms exports. Following a swift agreement within the Working Group, the meetings of the Councils of the European Communities (EC) in Luxembourg (June 1991) and Lisbon (June 1992) adopted a list of eight criteria to be considered before issuing export licenses (Council of the European Union 1991, 1992). Until then, member states had considered the acquisition and trade of armaments a restricted domain and relied on Article 223 of the Rome Treaty to protect what, for some of them, constituted a strategic part of their security policies and defence economies.

One impetus for heads of states and governments to change the regulation of arms exports were embarrassing revelations on arms exports to countries like Iraq. Another important factor was a changing defence sector. In light of shrinking demand and increasing production costs, the establishment of a common market came to be perceived as imperative to ensuring the survival of the arms industrial base in Western Europe (Walker and Gummett 1993; DeVestel 1995).

Following the adoption of the Luxembourg criteria, however, progress towards further regulations of the arms trade was stifled, in part, because of conflicting interests of the three major arms exporting countries: Germany; France; and Great Britain. Germany aimed for an ambitious and binding European-wide regulatory framework for arms sales that would preserve Germany's comparatively strict export control regime, while at the same time removing the strategic disadvantage that its armaments industry faced (Davis 2002: 93). In contrast, the traditional arms-exporting nations, France and Great Britain, were opposed to stringent Community-wide export rules for conventional weapons. Both believed that their commercial interests would be best served by maintaining the status quo. According to governmental representatives, the permission or denial of armament sales was so critical that it should rest with the nation state (ibid.: 55; Millar 1997). In light of such resistance, the eventual adoption of the Code of Conduct in 1998 came as a surprise to many. We show that, while NGOs played an important role in preparing the ground for the adoption of the Code by offering ideas and interpretations and forging coalitions, changes in the interests of key member states proved equally relevant.

NGO activism and the Code of Conduct

Already during the late 1980s, select NGOs had called for a 'moral order on the arms trade' in Europe with little effect. This changed with the adoption of the eight criteria. Although governments 'did not consider the [Luxembourg and Lisbon] criteria to be a first step towards a common policy on arms exports' (Cornish 1997: 79), they created opportunities for NGOs to build pressure for an EU-wide code on weapons sales.

Building on the Luxembourg criteria, a group of mostly British NGOs, including Saferworld, the World Development Movement, the British branch of Amnesty International (AI), and the British American Security Information Council (BASIC), started to develop and advocate proposals for an EU Code of Conduct. Convinced that the adoption of the eight criteria would remain ineffective as long as member states interpreted them differently and continued to keep information on their arms transfers confidential, the respective organizations, working on the national and the European level, called for both common interpretation and application of the criteria as well as the release of information on arms exports. Finally, to ensure the proper functioning of a European arms control export system, their proposals recommended a series of operating procedures, including the harmonization of licensing procedures, enhanced efforts to control the end-use of weapons, and the inclusion of both the European and national parliaments in controlling arms exports (Saferworld 1992: 10).

During this period, the European Parliament and the Commission served as *access points* for NGO input. The EP proved particularly receptive to Saferworld and others. Members of the European Parliament across party lines favoured a common approach to weapons sales and co-operation regarding armaments. They 'consistently exerted pressure for a more restrictive arms export control policy within the EU' from the early 1990s (Davis 2002: 94). Given their common interests, close ties developed between MEPs and NGOs. NGOs provided MEPs with valuable background information as well as practical and reliable proposals based on an intimate knowledge of the issues at stake, while MEPs kept NGOs informed about developments within the EU (Interviews 4 and 9, 2011).

Saferworld justified the need for a community-wide system primarily with *normative* arguments. It pointed, first, to the responsibility of arms-exporting EU states (Saferworld 1992: 2), and, second, to the growing recognition of the EU as a global actor and the impact it could consequently have on the creation of international norms and principles. The discursive strategies employed by Saferworld and other NGOs walked the fine line between softly criticizing governments and offering proposals for reform. On the one hand, the organizations used 'naming and shaming' to build pressure for an EU code by pointing to the discrepancies between the behaviour of EU member states regarding arms exports and the normative standards established by the eight criteria (Saferworld

1995). For example, in 1995 the World Development Movement released a report that documented how European countries violated the Luxembourg and Lisbon criteria concerning the 'respect of human rights in the final country of destination' by delivering arms to the Nigerian police despite its continuous suppression of pro-democracy demonstrations (United Press International 1995). On the other hand, however, NGOs devoted most of their energy to offering practical advice to policy-makers on how to improve existing European regulations. Building on its previous work of devising politically feasible elements for a Code, Saferworld, together with Amnesty International, BASIC, the World Development Organization and a team of international lawyers (Interview 1, 2011), composed a model code of conduct in 1995 (BASIC *et al.* 1995). Their draft included detailed provisions for the publication of transfers and denials, guidelines to prevent 'undercutting', a list of sensitive destinations, end-use provisions, arrangements for parliamentary scrutiny, and controls on arms brokering (UK Working Group on Arms 2010).

During this period, *Europeanization* remained fractured. While the reliance on expertise, consultation, and the delivery of concrete proposals for MEPs and like-minded state representatives worked well at the European level, it created schisms within the NGO community. Some of the grass-roots movements that pursued a more radical agenda, like the German-based Kampagne gegen Rüstungsexporte (Campaign against Arms Exports) or the British Campaign Against the Arms Trade (CAAT), distanced themselves from or left the NGO campaign for an EU Code of Conduct (Davis 2002: 99; Stavrianakis 2010: 77). Not only were some of these organizations frustrated with the process, which they felt was dominated by British NGOs (Stavrianakis 2010: 76), but they also favoured different solutions. Viewing a behavioural code as ineffective and inadequate, the respective organizations called for the termination of arms exports entirely, or proposed working towards the abolition of what they considered to be even more threatening types of arms, i.e., nuclear weapons (ibid.: 9). Some NGO representatives suggest that these radical positions helped the remaining NGOs in the long run (Interviews 1 and 2, 2011). Their criticism prompted the British-based organizations Saferworld and the World Development Movement, as well as the British chapters of Amnesty International and Oxfam, to extend their circle and mobilize support in other European countries.

In 1995 they launched a European-wide campaign calling for the establishment of an enforceable European code of conduct on arms exports (Davis 2002: 100). This campaign quickly took root. Within several months a network of over 600 NGOs across Europe supported the code. In addition, Saferworld and others lobbied governments across Europe. Aiming at co-ordinating the positions of like-minded states, they worked closely with governmental officials in COARM (Interview 1, 2011) and conducted expert seminars for senior civil servants (Anders 2005: 185). In addition to their transnational activities, the NGOs kept the pressure high at the national level, particularly in Great Britain, where the conservative government still opposed an EU code.

The activities of NGOs, directed at both the European and the national levels, began to take effect. In spring of 1997, the governments of Germany, Belgium, Ireland, the Netherlands and Sweden expressed their support for a restrictive arms export control regime together with 300 MEPs from eight member states (Saferworld 1997). Nevertheless, the impact of NGOs should not be overestimated. As representatives of the organizations involved themselves admit (Interviews 1, 2 and 3, 2011), changes in the calculations of key governments were critical and only fostered opportunities for civil society to become more involved in the process.

In particular Great Britain's move from being a vocal opponent of a code to being a fervent supporter proved decisive. This move followed a change in government from Tories to Labour. The latter had promised an 'ethical foreign policy' and to work for the introduction of a European code as part of a responsible arms trade during the party's election campaign (Millar 1997). Moreover, the British draft of European regulation mirrored the new national criteria for arms export licenses that the Labour government had adopted in response to the release of the so-called 'Scott report' concerning British arms sales to Iraq. Fearing a disadvantage in the international market, the British government tried to Europeanize its new export control policy. Shortly after the election, British NGOs formed the UK Working Group on Arms to ensure that the government would not only fulfil its election promise and establish a national code for arms exports, but at the same time assume leadership for an EU-wide code.

In addition to Great Britain, France became a co-supporter of the Code of Conduct, albeit for reasons that are less readily apparent. In official statements the French government also stressed ethical considerations (Carmona 1998: 17). These declarations were deliberate and sparked by negative public reactions to scandals, including the delivery of weapons to the Hutu regime until just before the genocide in Rwanda and to Iraq until shortly before the occupation of Kuwait. However, France's acquiescence also had other reasons. The government expected that the Code could be turned into a useful European instrument to fend off perceived American attempts to control and dominate the arms export policies of its allies (Sandrier and Martin 2000: 77). Moreover, given France's veto position in the Council of Ministers, French decision-makers counted on being able to control the composition of the Code. This calculation proved correct. As one observer remarks: 'In the face of threats by France to jeopardise the whole arrangement, all the weaker options [had been] chosen' (Davis 2002: 101).

Developments at the European level since the adoption of the EU Code of Conduct

In May 1998 the European foreign ministers adopted the EU Code of Conduct on Arms Exports, consisting of four parts. The first contains the preamble, and the second lists the eight Lisbon criteria. The third part stipulates the operative provisions according to which member states are obliged to inform each other about rejected arms export applications. In case a member state intends to substitute a denied transaction with an 'essentially identical transaction' (under-cut), it is required to consult with the member state(s) that had denied the arms transfer in first place. Should the undercutting country decide to go ahead with the transaction, it shall inform these (and only these) countries. The fourth part demands that member states compile and exchange information regarding their arms exports on a confidential basis. Building on these annual national reports, COARM would then prepare a consolidated version for the Council of Minis-ters. As a whole, the Code was conceived by member states as a voluntary, non-binding agreement, and the information they provided about armament sales was to be treated confidentially. Following its adoption, member states took several steps that seem counter intuitive, given the sensitivity of arms exports. We argue that NGOs were catalysts for and contributed significantly to the observed changes in the Code. The regulatory framework created additional access points at the European level and a moral standard on the basis of which civil society organizations could rhetorically entrap and hold govern-ments accountable. Before we discuss the role of NGOs in more detail, we will elaborate on the developments related to the Code of Conduct itself. Four are particularly noteworthy.

First, heads of states and governments began to develop more precise rules with respect to the application of the Code and by doing so decreased their room for discretion. For example, they defined central terms like 'essentially identical transactions' and clarified important issues, such as what constitutes a denial. These amendments to the Code were codified and published in the fourth and fifth annual reports of the Council in a Compendium of Agreed Practices (Council of the European Union 2002, 2003), which in 2004 was transformed into a continuously updated user's guide. Second, member states expanded the scope of the Code. While the original document applied to the shipment of tangible goods from Europe only, it now pertains to arms-broker-ing, transit transactions and the transfer of intangible technology, such as the shipment of blueprints via the Internet. They also developed a range of instru-ments to handle lifting previous EU arms embargoes. Third, in 2008 EU member states turned the Code into a binding agreement. This implies a legal obligation to harmonize their national legislation with the Code.

While these changes in the rules and scope of the Code of Conduct appear surprising, a fourth development, the growing amount of information that member states were willing to share both with each other (internal transparency) and their publics (external transparency) seems even more puzzling. With respect to internal transparency, EU governments moved: (1) from delivering reports to the Council that at first followed a 'home-made' structure to ones that adhered to common guidelines; (2) from providing rather little to deliver-ing more extensive information on their arms exports; and (3) from opposing to agreeing to the establishment of a central data pool in the Council Secretariat. In 2001, EU governments also decided that, in the case of an undercut, they would no longer only inform the original supplier country that had denied a transfer, but all member states instead (Bauer and Bromley 2004b: 16).

Regarding external transparency, member states agreed in 1999 to the publication of the consolidated Council report, something individual governments had vehemently rejected when the Code was first negotiated. Both the quantity and the quality of data provided in these reports increased from year to year. While the first consolidated report was just four pages long, the 2005 report contained 288 pages and provided much more detailed information. Furthermore, governments allowed greater EP involvement. Following a precedent set by the Finnish Presidency in 2001, it became accepted and common practice that Council Presidents would present the annually released consolidated report on arms exports to members of the Sub-Committee on Security and Defence and exchange views on the Code and related arms export issues with them. In the section on further progress in the seventh report, member states expressed their willingness to deepen this dialogue with the EP (Council of the European Union 2005: 10). Finally, member states also changed their national reporting systems. While in the late 1990s few of them published national reports on arms exports, most of them do now (Bromley 2008).

NGO activism and further development of the Code of Conduct

The *norms* established by the Code became a rallying point for civil society organizations. Defining what constituted acceptable or unacceptable state behaviour, the Code and its preamble provided a basis for NGOs to scandalize weapons sales that stood in clear violation of them. Furthermore, as a whole the Code allowed Saferworld, Amnesty International and others to draw attention to 'worrying gaps' and major shortcomings in the existing regime (Saferworld 2004). These included, among others, the lack of multilateral consultations in cases of denial, the Code's limited transparency – especially with respect to parliamentary accountability and scrutiny – and its non-binding character (Amnesty International *et al.* 1998).

Finally, drawing on both the guidelines accompanying the Code and the annual report released by the Council Secretariat, NGOs commented on governments' national reporting practices. For example, Saferworld published several in-depth studies in which the organization commended individual governments on their progress in enhancing transparency, but also pointed to discrepancies that continued to persist, particularly with respect to the quality of the reports and the scrutiny mechanisms. By asking, as one representative put it, uncomfortable questions, such as 'why [don't they] produce any information or report on this, while others do?' (Interview 2, 2011), NGOs set in motion 'beauty contests' among governments (Mariani and Urquhart 2000; Saferworld 2010). Initially merely conceived as a frame of reference, the Code of Conduct soon became a guide for good behaviour and an incentive for member states with already considerable transparency to submit 'good' or 'exemplary' reports. These type(s) of reports, in turn, pressured other governments, which had been reluctant to reveal information about their weapons export practices. Consequently, both the quantity and quality of data provided in the Council reports increased from year to year.

The institutionalization of the Code created additional *access points* for NGOs. As during the 1990s and in light of the newly established dialogue between Presidents and members of the Sub-Committee on Security and Defence, the EP remained an important gateway through which NGOs could channel their input into the political process. In addition, the parliamentary rapporteur for the Code, the Spanish MEP and former NGO activist Raül Romeva, constituted an important access point at least until recently when MEPs decided to abolish the position. Given that he was accepted by the member states and was informally invited to COARM meetings, he could channel viewpoints of NGOs into the decision-making process (Interview 9, 2011).

NGOs also established an institutionalized dialogue with the Council COARM working group. Ever since the Irish Presidency in the first semester of 2004, COARM–NGO meetings have taken place every autumn (Council of the European Union 2005: 3). Additionally, COARM holds a spring meeting with Saferworld. Discussions at COARM–NGO meetings usually concern operational issues. For example, the Bonn International Center for Conversion (BICC) was invited to present a data bank for licensing officers to assess the political situation in recipient countries based on the eight criteria of the Code (Interview 7, 2011). Confrontation or criticisms related to individual export decisions, by comparison, remain the exception at such meetings. In this respect, NGOs adjusted to the general working style within COARM meetings, where the national diplomats exchange first and foremost information related to technical matters, but refrain from discussing particular or politically sensitive cases (Interview 10, 2011).

Finally, individual EU Presidents proved receptive to input by NGOs. For example, when the Dutch government declared the harmonization of national reporting as one of its priorities during its EU Presidency, it asked the renowned Swedish International Peace Research Institute (SIPRI) to compile a report on the deficiencies of the existing national reporting systems and ways to improve it (Gemeinsame Konferenz Kirche und Entwicklung 2004: 38; Bauer and Bromley 2004a, 2004b). And when the Dutch government launched a discussion within COARM on the interpretation of the eighth criterion of the Code on development, it tasked the Dutch branch of Oxfam to provide data and prepare a study on its proper handling and interpretation. At the suggestion of the Dutch delegation, Oxfam was even invited to present results of the study at the COARM meeting (Interviews 1 and 8, 2011). While the Dutch Presidency might be regarded as exceptional as far as armament-related interactions between NGOs and governments are concerned, consultations with civil organizations prior to a government's presidential tenure have become, as already mentioned, almost common practice even on issues related to foreign and security policy and maybe, as we will show in the case of France and Spain, even consequential (Interview 2, 2011).

Congruent with the co-evolution thesis, we observe a *Europeanization* effect. The formerly British-dominated NGO coalition has transformed into a European-wide network comprised of groups and organizations such as the Quaker Council of European Affairs, the Groupe de Recherche et d'Information sur la Paix et la Sécurité (GRIP), the Flemish Peace Institute in Belgium, SIPRI, BICC, the Joint Conference Church and Development, and the Dutch Campaign against Arm Trade. Moreover, the national branches of constituency-based organizations became involved.

For example, while prior to the Code the participation of Amnesty International or Oxfam was limited to their British sections, following its adoption the French and Spanish became involved. Although most of these groups are still rooted at the national level, they are connected at the European level, coordinate policy and inform their national audiences about European developments. These cross-level interdependencies added to the strength and leverage of NGOs *vis-à-vis* governments.

Network members fed developments at the European level or in other states into national debates and simultaneously reported national decisions and relevant information on arms exports back to the European level. For example, while the early reports of the German Joint Conference Church and Development focused exclusively on German arms exports and export regulations, later reports contained chapters on European developments as well. More importantly, NGOs ensured that the Code became a reference point in national debates. When criticizing their government for contravening the principles of the Code, French NGOs, for example, referred to good practices in other states for leverage and by doing so successfully nudged responsible ministries, as a recent case study illustrates, towards providing more information on arms exports (Dembinski and Schumacher 2005: 31–5) and reversing their positions. Oxfam France, working together with other national and European NGOs and networks, launched a campaign that shifted the balance in the French government from initial opposition to supporting a legally binding Code of Conduct (Oxfam France 2008). According to one participant, 'it was an opportune time' (Interview 3, 2011). Given that France was about to take over the EU presidency, 'it would have been a major embarrassment for the French government as a co-founder of the Code, to be portrayed as anti-European and not to agree to the Common Position' (ibid.). Moreover, French NGOs received support from like-minded governments in the COARM group where it became increasingly tough for France to maintain its position. Linkages between national NGOs and EU networks also resulted in some cases in changes in national law.

In Spain, for example, four NGOs – Amnistía Internacional, Greenpeace, Intermón Oxfam and Medicos sin Fronteras – launched a campaign in 2001/2 entitled 'Farewell to Arms' which, though primarily aimed at the control of small arms and light weapons, culminated in the adoption of an exemplary arms export law in 2007 (Bromley 2008: 43). The organizations involved successfully engaged in a two-level game. On the one hand, they put pressure on the Spanish representative of COARM to become a spokesperson for, among other things, increased transparency rules at the EU level, European-wide regulations of arms-brokering, and of licensed production overseas (Amnistía Internacional *et al.* 2002). On the other hand, NGOs used the Code of Conduct on Arms Exports together with what they perceived as best practice in other EU states as a lobbying tool to exact of the Spanish government far-reaching transparency and reporting rules.

CONCLUSION

Our analysis of the Code of Conduct demonstrates that research on the EU's CFSP could profit from a governance turn. More specifically, we show that NGOs and transnational NGO networks take part and have an influence on the development of the European arms export control regime. Concurrent with established patterns, we find that the Europeanization of arms export regulations increased voice opportunities of NGOs. The adoption of the Lisbon criteria in 1991 and of the Code in 1998, in particular, created incentives for these organizations to mobilize at the European level. They established new access points and allowed them to exploit European norms. While NGOs exerted pressure from above and below on member states, our case study shows that they preferred insider strategies at the European level and tended to engage in symbolic action at the national level.

With respect to arms exports, observers and practitioners agree that without the pressure and blueprints of NGOs the adoption of the EU Code of Conduct would have certainly taken longer and the regulatory framework most probably looked very different. Although the volume of arms exports and the actual licensing practices have changed very little, governments today have to, as one NGO representative put it, 'jump through more hoops before exporting arms to difficult destinations' (Interview 2, 2011).

What are the implications of our findings for the CFSP as a policy and as a democratic system? Our research suggests that policy-making in the second pillar seems no longer as opaque and as state-centric as the standard literature assumes. While decisions related to the European-wide regulatory system were certainly taken in camera, it was nevertheless possible for NGOs to obtain information related to these. Sympathetic states, MEPs and individual EU Presidencies were important linking pins through which NGOs could stay abreast with ongoing discussions or channel their ideas. Moreover, formal and informal rules or practices and their unintended consequences facilitated the involvement of civil society organizations and other actors. The provisions of the Code provided arguments to hold governments accountable and standards against which to judge their behaviour. Finally, in the case of the Code, NGOs and their networks themselves are a reason why the characterization of the CFSP as intergovernmental appears inappropriate. Select organizations have established themselves as experts whose judgments could not be easily dismissed by states and who successfully contributed to the emergence of a public space transcending national boundaries and expanding to the European level.

At first sight, the involvement of NGOs in the formulation of foreign policy may be taken as encouraging signs and as a movement toward a more democratic CFSP. Nevertheless, there are some caveats one needs to consider. Many of the NGOs which specialize in security issues and are active at the European level are more akin to think-tanks than constituency-based organizations; they specialize in the provision of well-researched information, policy-advising, and consultation. Therefore it can be questioned whether and to what extent these organizations are representative of or can speak for those either negatively affected by or opposed to arms exports. Furthermore, at the same time as these organizations potentially contribute to more transparency or different policy outcomes at the supranational level, they also lend legitimacy to governments and European decision-making. Soliciting the views of NGOs also may serve governments as a shield, insofar as they can justify actions and policies by referring to the seal of approval from civil society. Both of these concerns have been raised in the first pillar as well. They therefore may be a further sign that the CFSP is becoming more akin to other policy areas. Yet, they should not detract from the positive developments that can be attributed to NGOs.

Biographical notes: Jutta Joachim is a Professor of International Relations at the University of Hannover in Germany. Matthias Dembinski is a Member of the Executive Board of the Peace Research Institute Frankfurt (PRIF).

ACKNOWLEDGEMENTS

We would like to thank Helene Sjursen, Sophie Vanhoonacker, the anonymous reviewers, and the participants of the Eurotrans Workshop for their helpful comments; and Natalia Dalmer for her research assistance. We would also like to thank the NGO representatives, state and EU officials who agreed to be interviewed.

NOTE

1 Although scholars have studied Europe's defence industry (e.g., Guay 1997; Guay and Callum 2002) and the interactions between interest and civil society groups on the one hand and EU governments on the other in the lead-up to international agreements such as, for example, the Kyoto Protocol (e.g., Oberthür 1999) or the Rome Statute in 2000 establishing the International Criminal Court (e.g., Deitelhoff 2009), their role in EU policy-making is not well understood. More recent standard works on the CFSP fail to mention NGOs (e.g., Cameron 2007; Howarth 2007; Keukeleire and MacNaughtan 2008; Smith 2009) just as those on interest representation in the EU omit chapters on foreign and security policy (e.g., Warleigh and Fairbrass 2002; Greenwood 2003).

REFERENCES

Amnesty International, BASIC, Christian Aid, Oxfam, Saferworld and World Development Movement (1998) *Final Analysis. EU Code of Conduct on the Arms Trade*, June 1998.

Amnistía Internacional, Greenpeace, Intermón Oxfam and Medicos sin Fronteras (2002) *A Responsible European Policy on Arms Transfers*, January 2002.

Anders, H. (2005) 'NGOs and the shaping of the European controls on arms exports', in E. Krahmann (ed.), *New Threats and New Actors in Security Governance*, Basingstoke: Palgrave Macmillan.

BASIC, Saferworld and World Development Movement (1995) *A European Code of Conduct on the Arms Trade*, London.

Bauer, S. and Bromley, M. (2004a) 'The EU Code of Conduct on Arms Exports: enhancing the accountability of arms exports policies', *European Security* 12: 129–47.

Bauer, S. and Bromley, M. (2004b) 'The European Union Code of Conduct on Arms Exports: improving the Annual Report', *SIPRI Policy Paper 8*, Stockholm: Stockholm International Peace Research Institute.

Bayne, S. and Trolliet, P. (2009), 'Stocktaking and scoping of the Peacebuilding Partnership', Study for the European Commission – DG RELEX A/2, available at http://ec.europa.eu/external_relations/ifs/pbp_en.htm (accessed 7 April 2011).

Börzel, T.A. and Risse, T. (2003) 'Conceptualizing the domestic impact of Europe', in K. Featherstone and C.M. Radaelli (eds), *The Politics of Europeanization*, Oxford: Oxford University Press, pp. 57–82.

Bromley, M. (2008) 'The impact on domestic policy of the EU Code on Arms Exports: the Czech Republic, the Netherlands, and Spain', *SIPRI Policy Paper 21*, Stockholm: Stockholm International Peace Research Institute.

Cameron, F. (2007) *An Introduction to European Foreign Policy*, London and New York: Routledge.

Carmona, R. (1998) 'Un Code de Bonne Conduite pour les Exportations d'Armements', *Défense en France* 8(9): 171–5.

Cornish, P. (1997) 'Joint action, "The Economic Aspects of Security" and the regulation of conventional arms and technology exports from the EU', in M. Holland (ed.), *Common Foreign and Security Policy. The Record and Reforms*, London: Pinter.

Council of the European Union (1991) 'Declaration on non-proliferation and arms exports', *Bulletin-EG 6-1991*, Brussels and Luxembourg, 29 June.

Council of the European Union (1992) 'European Council, Lisbon, June 26–27', *Bulletin-EG 6-1992*, Brussels and Luxembourg.

Council of the European Union (1998) 'European Code of Conduct on Arms Exports', *8675/2/98 Rev. 2*, Brussels, 3 June.

Council of the European Union (2002) 'Fourth annual report according to Operative Provision 8 of the European Code of Conduct on Arms Exports', *13779/02*, Brussels, 11 November.

Council of the European Union (2003) 'Fourth annual report according to Operative Provision 8 of the European Code of Conduct on Arms Exports', 14712/03, Brussels, 26 November.

Council of the European Union (2005) 'Seventh annual report according to Operating Provision 8 of the European Union Code of Conduct on Arms Exports', *14053/05*, Brussels, 14 November.

Council of the European Union (2008) 'Council Joint Action 2008/230/CFSP of 17 March 2008', *Official Journal of the European Union*, L75-L85, 18 March, Brussels.

Davis, I. (2002) *The Regulation of Arms and Dual-Use Exports. Germany, Sweden and the UK*, Oxford: Oxford University Press.

Deitelhoff, N. (2009) 'The discursive process of legalization: charting islands of persuasion in the ICC case', *International Organization* 63(1): 33–65.

Dembinski, M. (2009) 'NGOs and security: the case of the European Union', in J. Joachim and B. Locher (eds), *Transnational Activism in the UN and the EU. A Comparative Study*, London and New York: Routledge, pp. 154–68.

Dembinski, M. and Schumacher, B. (2005) 'Wie Europa dem Rüstungsexport Schranken Setzt: Von der Zusammenarbeit europäischer Regierungen zum europäischen Regieren', *HSFK Report no. 9*, Frankfurt am Main: Hessische Stiftung Friedens- und Konfliktforschung.

DeVestel, P. (1995) 'Defence markets and industries in Europe: time for political decisions?', *Chaillot Paper no. 21*, Paris: The European Institute for Security Studies.

Eichener, V. and Voelzkow, H. (1994) *Europäische Integration und Verbandliche Interessenvermittlung. Ko-Evolution von politisch-administrativem System und Verbändelandschaft*, Marburg: Metropolis-Verlag.

European Peacebuilding Liaison Office (2011) 'Civil society dialogue network', available at http://www.eplo.org/civilsociety-dialogue-network.html (accessed 7 April 2011).

Featherstone, K. (2003) 'Introduction: in the name of "Europe"', in K. Featherstone and C.M. Radaelli (eds), *The Politics of Europeanization*, Oxford: Oxford University Press, pp. 3–26.

Gemeinsame Konferenz Kirche und Entwicklung (2004) *Rüstungsexportbericht 2004*, Berlin.

Gourlay, C. (2006) *Partners Apart. Enhancing Cooperation between Civil Society and EU Civilian Crisis Management in the Framework of ESDP*, Jyväskylä: CMI, EPLO and KATU.

Greenwood, J. (2003) *Interest Representation in the European Union*, New York: Palgrave Macmillan.

Greenwood, J. (2009) 'Institutions and civil society organizations in the EU's multilevel system', in J. Joachim and B. Locher (eds), *Transnational Activism in the UN and the EU. A Comparative Study*, London and New York: Routledge, pp. 93–104.

Guay, T.R. (1997) 'The European Union, expansion of policy-making, and defense industrial policy', *Journal of European Public Policy* 4(3): 404–21.

Guay, T.R. and Callum, R. (2002) 'The transformation and future prospects of Europe's defence industry', *International Affairs* 78(4): 757–76.

Howarth, J. (2007) *Security and Defence Policy in the European Union*, Basingstoke: Palgrave Macmillan.

Keck, M.E. and Sikkink, K. (1998) *Activists Beyond Borders. Advocacy Networks in International Politics*, Ithaca, NY, and London: Cornell University Press.

Keukeleire, S. and MacNaughtan, J. (2008) *The Foreign Policy of the European Union*, Basingstoke: Palgrave Macmillan.

Kirchner, E. (2006) 'The challenge of European Union security governance', *Journal of Common Market Studies* 44(5): 947–68.

Kohler-Koch, B. (1996) 'Die Gestaltungsmacht organisierter Interessen', in M. Jachtenfuchs and B. Kohler-Koch (eds), *Europäische Integration*, Opladen: Leske and Budrich, pp. 193–224.

Kohler-Koch, B. and Rittberger, B. (2006) 'Review article: the "governance turn" in EU studies', *Journal of Common Market Studies* 44: 27–49.

Krahmann, E. (2003) *Multilevel Networks in European Foreign Policy*, Aldershot: Ashgate.

Mariani, B. and Urquhart, A. (2000) 'Transparency and accountability in European arms export controls. Towards common standards and best practice', *Saferworld Report*, London: Saferworld.

Mérand, F., Hofmann, S.C. and Irondelle, B. (2010) 'Transgovernmental networks in European security and defence policy', in S. Vanhoonacker, H. Dijkstra and H. Maurer (eds), 'Understanding the role of bureaucracy in the European security and defence policy', *European Integration online Papers (EIoP)*, Special Issue 1, vol. 14, available at http://eiop.or.at/eiop/pdf/2010-005.pdf (accessed 30 March 2011).

Millar, D. (1997) 'Human rights: NGOs urge European code of conduct on arms sales', *IPS-Inter Press Service*, 6 March.

Oberthür, S. (1999) 'The EU as an international actor: the case of the protection of the ozone layer', *Journal of Common Market Studies* 37(4): 641–59.

Oxfam France (2008) '2008: Le Contrôle des Armes à Portée de Main', Oxfam France, available at http://www.oxfamfrance.org/2008-Le-controle-des-armes-a,265?lang=en (accessed 5 April 2011).

Pierre, J. (2000) 'Introduction: understanding governance', in J. Pierre (ed.), *Debating Governance. Authority, Steering and Democracy*, Oxford: Oxford University Press, pp. 1–12.

Rummel, R. (2003) 'EU Friedenspolitik durch Konfliktprävention: Erfahrungen mit dem Conflict Prevention Network', in P. Schlotter (ed.), *Europa-Macht-Frieden? Zur Politik der Zivilmacht Europa*, Baden-Baden: Nomos, pp. 240–77.

Saferworld (1992) 'Arms and dual-use exports from the EC: a common policy for regulation and control', *Saferworld Report*, London: Saferworld.

Saferworld (1995) 'Proliferation and export controls', *Saferworld Report*, London: Saferworld.

Saferworld (1997) 'Update', *Saferworld Report*, London: Saferworld.

Saferworld (2004) 'Taking control. The case for a more effective European Union Code of Conduct on Arms Exports: a report by non-governmental organizations', *Saferworld Report*, London: Saferworld.

Saferworld (2010) 'More than box-ticking? Arms transfer reporting in the EU', *Saferworld Report*, London: Saferworld.

Sandrier, J.C. and Martin, C.A. (2000) 'Veyret, Rapport d'Information sur le Control des Exportations d'Armement', *Assemblée Nationale, No. 2334.4/2000*, available at http://www.assemblee-nationale.fr/legislatures/11/pdf/rap-info/i2334.pdf (accessed 30 March 2011).

Schmitt, B. (2000) 'From cooperation to integration: defence and aerospace industries in Europe', *Chaillot Paper No. 40*, Paris: The European Union Institute for Security Studies.

Sicurelli, D. (2008) 'Framing security and development in the EU pillar structure: how the views of the European Commission affect EU Africa policy', *Journal of European Integration* 30(2): 217–34.

Smith, K.E. (2009) *European Union Foreign Policy in a Changing World*, Cambridge, MA: Polity Press.

Stavrianakis, A. (2010) *Taking Aim at the Arms Trade*, London and New York: Zed Books.

Stone Sweet, A. and Sandholtz, W. (1997) 'European integration and supranational governance', *Journal of European Public Policy* 4(3): 297–317.

UK Working Group on Arms (2010) *An EU Code of Conduct on the Arms Trade: Essential Standards*, London: UK Working Group on Arms.

United Press International (1995) 'Pressure grows to ban arms to Nigeria', *United Press International*, 11 June.

Vanhoonacker, S., Dijkstra, H. and Maurer, H. (2010) 'Understanding the role of bureaucracy in the European security and defence policy: the state of the art', in S. Vanhoonacker, H. Dijkstra and H. Maurer (eds), 'Understanding the Role of Bureaucracy in the European Security and Defence Policy', *European Integration online Papers (EIoP)*, Special Issue 1, vol. 14, available at http://eiop.or.at/eiop/index.php/eiop/article/viewFile/2010_004a/180 (accessed 30 March 2011).

Walker, W. and Gummett, P. (1993) *Nationalism, Internationalism and the European Defense Market*, Paris: Institute for Security Studies of the Western European Union.

Warleigh, A. and Fairbrass, J. (2002) *Influence and Interests in the European Union. The New Politics of Persuasion, Advocacy and Influence*, London: Europa Publications.

Webber, M., Croft, S., Howorth, J., Terriff, T. and Krahmann, E. (2004) 'The governance of European security', *Review of International Studies* 30: 3–26.

Governance between expertise and democracy: the case of European Security

Erik Oddvar Eriksen

ABSTRACT The European Union (EU) constitutes a multifarious security environment in which the demand for expert knowledge is on the rise. The objective of securing the sound specialized knowledge required for the EU's so-called *comprehensive security strategy* may not meet the requirement of being democratically accountable. There is hardly any objective knowledge basis for 'experts' in this field and different knowledge systems are connected to different validation and accountability procedures. A comprehensive security policy would blur the institutional and legal boundaries of the constitutional state. The deliberative approach to democratic governance offers some prescripts for achieving a comprehensive security policy involving humanitarian and civilian aspects alongside the military and technological ones. But deliberation cannot bear the burden of democratic legitimation.

INTRODUCTION

In security politics, more than in any policy area, we seem to be in the hands of experts. Prior to the invasion of Iraq we depended on them in order to find out about 'weapons of mass destruction'. The UK government's dossier on the Iraq issue famously stated that 'Iraq could launch chemical or biological weapons within 45 minutes of an order to do so'.[1] This shows all too well that knowledge is fallible and that expertise is erroneous.

How can the citizens know that decisions which affect them are not made on the basis of biased information and how can they control that the scientific community is not pursuing its own interests to the detriment of the public interest? History is replete with examples of politically biased information and incorrect propositions in foreign and security policy-making. Moreover, how can we know that decisions are based on the right premises when only a few, for *security reasons*, have access to all information?

A further problem with regard to balancing the need for expertise and accountability in the security field is particular to the European Union (EU).

101

In the multilevel constellation that makes up the EU, this policy field is very much in need of the knowledge of researchers from different disciplines. The security challenges resulting from 9/11 have led to an increased demand for a broader span of knowledge as well as a larger role of intelligence in decision-making. The attacks by international jihadists on 11 March 2004 in Madrid and 7 July 2005 in London made clear that also Europe was a target. But expertise, if it can deliver truth at all, cannot deliver it in a coherent way when many 'sciences' are involved, and is open for political manipulation. Hence the question: is the increasing demand for scientific expertise in the field of security policy necessarily a good thing? The problem is exacerbated by the EU's focus on the so-called *comprehensive security concept.*

In 2000 the EU embarked upon a process of improving the link between knowledge and security policy, and also between the various components of research in order for it to be better equipped to face new and unprecedented security challenges. The ensuing comprehensive security concept involves humanitarian and civilian aspects alongside military and technological ones. The European Security Strategy (ESS) (Council of the European Union 2003) identifies five dimensions of threat: terrorism; organized crime; failing states; proliferation of weapons of mass destruction; and regional conflict. The ESS was revised in 2008 to include non-strategic threats such as cyber-security, climate change and pandemics. These dimensions have very different cognitive cores and normative and legal standings. When these are merged there is a danger of blurring institutional and legal boundaries. The comprehensive security concept raises particular concerns with regard to the formal demands of a democratic *Rechtsstaat* according to which accountability as well as the legal protection of individual rights must be ensured, concerns that also were raised by the Commission.[2] One may, however, ask whether the particular governance character of the EU – its so-called '*sui generis*' status – calls for different standards of accountability. Even when it comes to security, governance is on the agenda in the EU (Krahmann 2003; Webber *et al.* 2004). Security governance depicts a problem-solving scheme in which governmental and non-governmental actors act on the basis of a consented knowledge base.

I will address the relationship between scientific expertise and democracy with regard to the ambiguity of a comprehensive and accountable security agenda. Ensuring the sound specialized knowledge required for a comprehensive security policy may collide with the accountability requirement. Different knowledge systems are connected to different validation procedures, which makes accountability tricky. However, can new *forms of governance* premised on informalism and deliberative practice solve the problem of technocracy: that experts have the upper hand in political decision-making? I argue that while the deliberative approach to multilevel governance offers some prescripts for achieving a comprehensive security policy, it is found wanting in normative terms.

This contribution analyses the democratic deficiencies of technocracy and governance. Further, it discusses the potential remedy by making governance more deliberative, criticizing the latter from a specific deliberative perspective.

I start by discussing how the problem of technocracy haunts modern policy-making as well as the EU's multifarious security environment in which the traditional, hierarchical model of democratic accountability has become obsolete. Subsequently, I address whether new governance structures can, in principle, alleviate the problem.

PART I: EPISTOCRATIC DOMINANCE

Science or politics?

The problematic relationship between knowledge and political decision-making has ridden students of politics since the days of Plato. To him there was no dilemma. Plato famously argued that the wisest should rule because of their knowledge of *the good*. But in a democracy all should have an equal say with regard to what is good and just, and scientific knowledge is often contested. Epistocracy – rule of the experts, the knowers – is illegitimate according to the democratic credo because we can only know what is good and just by hearing the affected parties.

However, knowledge based on truth claims is indispensable in modern policy-making. No government can make viable decisions without knowledge of facts, causal connections and interconnections as well as of risk estimates and possible negative effects of measures. Thus, the problem of epistocracy is not over with the establishment of the democratic *Rechtsstaat*. The problem of 'the rule of knowers' is even more present in foreign and security policy, which has traditionally been the prerogative of the executive. This policy field is steadily becoming more demanding with regard to knowledge. In the wake of 9/11 an increasingly independent network of security experts has been on the rise. The EU now routinely uses expert advice for its security policy initiatives. Its multilevel structure of governing and the multifarious security field make it hard to pinpoint whether it is politicians or experts who have the upper hand in policy-making. Moreover, in the field of security one may ask who can count as an expert.

The EU has embarked upon a process of implementing a *comprehensive security concept* and what is termed Civil–Military Co-ordination. It has to be seen in the context of a growth in security provisions by the EU by means of civilian and military crisis operations under the Common Security and Defence Policy (CSDP), as well as in a context of a changing security environment (Gross 2008). But what is scientific or objective knowledge of security issues? This question is even more pertinent when it comes to the *comprehensive* security strategy, which is the key characteristic of the EU's approach to security. It calls for a mixture of competences from the fields of intelligence, military, judicial, policing, as well as regional, local, political and economic expertise. It is difficult to speak of specialized, objective knowledge in a field that is so infused with value judgments, and where research is often intimately linked to the so-called military industrial complex and their particular interests and perspectives. This is, however, a general problem facing modern policy-making.

Epistocratic dominance

Since the dawn of social science, one has questioned whether or not the development of modern expertise and its involvement with democratic government has set aside the whole idea of citizens' collective self-rule. Already Henri de Saint-Simon (1975 [1760–1825]) posed the question of science precedence. Max Weber (1921) famously counterpoised the role of the expert to that of the politician. In his model expertise provides the government with the required knowledge about which means to select in order to reach a political goal; this is so to say inherent in the epistemology of modern science as well as in the principle of the value-neutral bureaucracy. They are constituted on distinctions between is and ought, facts and norms, administration and politics. Experts deal with *means* based on verified knowledge and politicians (or citizens) with *goals* based on norms and values. The establishment of knowledge-based administrative staff, with competences delimited and compartmentalized in a norm hierarchy, provides political authorities with a powerful instrument for goal attainment. The politicians make use of objective knowledge established by science – knowledge of which means would be good or bad for reaching a specific goal.

One need not follow Weber's decisionistic approach, where normative questions are seen as rationally irresolvable, to see his model as the exemplary of the democratic *Rechtsstaat*. One could even formulate the essence of this model in a deliberative theoretical manner: the experts take part in a reciprocal political discourse, in which they on the one hand give advice to politicians prior to decision-making, and on the other hand respond to representatives' request for scientific assessments of proposals and claims. The experts' role is then confined to a scientific or advisory one, subordinate to the politicians who uphold their main position as responsible policy-makers who are accountable to the citizenry through public debate and elections – all within the legal constraints that apply. In this model experts are needed to support the policy-makers with the necessary data and probability assessments in order to qualify decisions so that they can endure public scrutiny and harsh criticism. The danger is that the serving scientific machinery becomes the real master.

As the modern system of science developed and was connected to modern administration, both directly through the establishment of own bodies of competence as well as indirectly through research institutions, a growing body of knowledge for decision-making accumulated. The upshot was a science-based technology premised on validated data and a system in which research and technology are tightly interwoven with the economy and administration (Habermas 1969: 71). Hence, the allegation of *technocracy*. According to Jacques Ellul (1954), the relationship between expertise and political leadership is turned on its head. Echoing Saint-Simon, he argued that scientific expertise is the *hegemon*. It forces politicians to choose particular solutions because of documented matters of fact.

In the post-war period, the Cold War climate, the conspiracy environment and the atomic threat justified secrecy and large zones of discretion and little public accountability. It created a fertile ground for technocratic politics. The establishment of compound research institutions and their production of new problem-solving methods led to new options. Experts were able to pinpoint new strategies for goal attainment. This implied that the relationship between expertise and decision-making was inverted. Increasingly, science produced solutions to problems that were not (yet) politically articulated, and increasingly it found solutions that appeared to be *necessary*: they stem from the nature of the things themselves. According to Helmut Schelsky (1961), empirical laws supplanted political will formation. The specialists won through new techniques and methods that rationalized decision-making to the point where politicians only nominally keep on being decision-makers. The space for political decision-making decreased. The real power was in the hands of the scientific expertise. Popular sovereignty became subordinated science, because the complexity of issues called for expert knowledge. It was government *for* the people, not by the people. However, is really complexity in itself an argument against democracy?

Complexity revisited

The answer is no. Democracy could not prevail without division of labour, specialization, and without representation and the legal walls between state and society as well as between legislative, judiciary and executive powers. Without such walls the level of personal freedom and intelligent decision-making that we witness in modern society would not exist (Bohman 1996: 162). The build-up of competences, the institutionalization of bodies of specialized formal knowledge and the contest between different expert systems, furnishes decision-makers with information and increases the level of knowledge as well as the obligation to provide reasons.

Moreover, such arrangements represent effective barriers to *over-democratization* – to thrusting lay participation to solve intricate problems – and to hyper-rationality (Dahrendorf 1974; Elster 2007: 214). There are no illusions that all types of questions can be solved through lay participation and public deliberation. Some questions require advanced knowledge and highly specialized expertise in order to be solved properly. This is an argument for seeing public opinion- and will-formation as a mode of democratic rule, reserved for some types of questions, not all, and to see corporatist, epistemic communities and deliberative bodies as necessary supplements to ordinary politics (cp. Habermas 1996: 305). Complicated questions require complicated answers. Not all problems can be, nor should they be, solved through lay participation and public deliberations. One may argue that there is a political division of labour; and that science-based expertise possesses a justified space of action in modern societies. This is so because we cannot know whether empirical assertions are true unless all arguments are aired – and in modern societies only the scientific community is held to be able to test truth claims.

When it comes to whether a normative claim is warranted or not, we cannot know unless all affected parties have been consulted. Hence, the democratic *principle of reciprocity*: 'The moral claims that citizens make must be justifiable with reference to principles and reasons that are mutually acceptable' (Gutmann and Thompson 1996: 55). What, then, about the *secrecy* that security demands? The principle of reciprocal justification does not require democratic deliberation at every stage of decision-making processes as long as the principles for secrecy themselves are justified at some point in a deliberative process. As long as the principles and guidelines for secrecy are publicly debated and regulated, actors may operate, within given parameters, in secrecy without violating democratic norms. Hence, the field of foreign and security policy is not exempted from the rules of the democratic game.

Complexity demands and secrecy do not, then, amount to an argument against democracy. To the contrary, without scientific clarification of facts and arguments, the epistemic quality of decisions would not be good enough to engender mass approval. But, as indicated, an appropriate relationship presupposes that facts and values can be neatly separated. This is not easy in the security field in which facts are infused with values and considerations of feasibility. Under proper conditions deliberation disentangles facts and values. It contributes to the rationality of decision-making by the pooling of information and by argumentatively testing the reasons presented (Goodin 2005: 91ff). The deliberative perspective also helps clarify a second requirement for proper relationships between expertise and politics, that of democratic accountability.

Autonomy and accountability

Deliberation is the answer to the requirement that those affected by laws and policies should be given justifications. In this way the equality of citizens is respected. Moreover, only by justifying the decisions to those affected by them, and involving them in a dialogue, is there reason to believe that they are correct. Democracy is thus a claim of justice but *institutions* are needed to meet this requirement. The minimal institutional design consists of: (a) the *rule-of-law principle*, which guarantees the equal protection of individuals; (b) *rights to political participation* including egalitarian procedures of decision-making; and (c) *state-free spaces* in the civil society constituted by communication and association rights. This design is meant to ensure both the liberal principle of liberty and the republican principle of popular sovereignty, which respectively warrant the private and the public autonomy of citizens.

The basic normative standards with regard to which political orders can claim legitimacy, and from which the above principles are derived, are those of *autonomy* and *accountability*. By autonomy is meant the basic democratic principle that those affected by laws should also be authorized to make them. Intrinsic to this criterion is the possibility of the authorized bodies of decision-making to react adequately on public support to determine the development of the political community in such a way that the citizens can be seen to act upon themselves (Eriksen 2009: 35). Accountability designates a relationship in which the decision-makers can be held responsible to the citizenry, and wherein, in the last resort, it is possible to dismiss incompetent rulers. Accountability rests on the foundation of the public's right to get proper justifications for the actions of officials and professionals as officials (Dowdle 2006: 3). It requires more than report, control, transparency and openness. Accountability refers to a relationship that is multilateral rather than unilateral, dialogical rather than monological. It is deliberative as it involves two-way communication between the representative and the represented, who both ask questions and give answers (Mansbridge 2009: 384). Accountability is 'a relationship between an actor and a forum, in which the actor has an obligation to explain and to justify his or her conduct, the forum can pose questions and pass judgment, and the actor may face consequences' (Bovens 2007: 467; see also Harlow 2002). The 'rock bottom' of accountability is an *obligation to provide good arguments for one's judgments*, decisions and actions to the public. It is a three-fold predicate: decision-makers are answerable to *someone* – who can hold them to account – for *something* that can be rendered account of. This 'something' may be right or wrong, good or bad, hence it can be assessed according to inter-subjective standards – be they professional ethical standards or political–legal ones. Accountability is thus an *epistemic concept*. The core of accountability is justification and the core of justification is good arguments.

It is difficult to meet this requirement when the knowledge base is diverse: who should answer the pertinent questions on the basis of which knowledge? The more complex the knowledge base, the more difficult it is to locate the locus of accountability, and to hold decision-makers to account. This is the case with the security field where the composite character of knowledge is a core feature. Another complication is that scientific knowledge itself is thrown into doubt.

PART II: THE GOVERNANCE AGENDA

Risk and normativity

The agenda for science-based policy-making has changed since the heyday of value freedom and scientific optimism. Science is no longer perceived as an innocent instrument in realizing political goals. At least since the Chernobyl catastrophe, science has come to be seen as a co-producer of risks (Beck 1986). In the EU, the Mad Cow Disease (BSE) and other food scandals,[3] and the ensuing critique of the European Food Safety Agency (EFSA), marked a watershed with regard to trust in science. Scientific knowledge gives itself away as contradictory and risky. Its effects can be negative, not solely positive for the environment, and scholarly based intelligence needed for military operations, for security and defence, has often turned out to be wrong or biased.

Nevertheless, the need for security-relevant knowledge in a situation of increased risks has been spurred by the speedy development of a European security architecture. Also the European Parliament (2011) underlines the need for expertise. Viable solutions require expert knowledge based on verified scientific data including calculating hazards and assessing probabilities as to what harm an event could cause.

In 2001 the Commission adopted a 'Science and Society Action Plan' that aimed at establishing a 'new partnership' between science and society. Guidelines were published in a Communication in December 2002 (European Commission 2002). Further, in 2004 the Commission published a communication entitled *European security research*; in this it brought together the demands and suppliers of research and technology in a 50-person-strong board. The European Security Research Advisory Board (ESRAB) was established in 2005. In addition to five members of the European Parliament and representatives from the European Commission services, it consisted of high-level specialists and strategists including public authorities, industry, research institutions and specialist think-tanks. The EU responded to their request for more security research with two seven-year Framework Programmes in the Area of Security over the 2007–2013 period.[4]

The security field is crowded with expertise and counter expertise. Networks of intelligence and (in)security professions compete over the definition of what constitutes risk and over who can claim to know better than others (Bigo 2006). Moreover, risk assessment, which goes to the core of the security agenda, pertains to normatively charged decisions affecting lives and shaping our common future. Whether a certain level of risk is acceptable or not cannot be determined through purely scientific means, and has been the object of continued controversy over the years (Joerges *et al.* 1997; Fischer 2009). Further testimony to the value-ladenness and normativity of risk assessment is the fact that, in a constitutional state, such assessment has never been delegated in its entirety to expert bodies.

In political controversies in general truth claims are interwoven with moral and counterfactual claims. For example, when experts advise politicians whether to vaccinate against pandemics, this has less to do with the actual facts than with responsibility and socially defined standards of health. The same can be said about the arguments for invading Iraq; they reflected standards of human protection and not merely 'objective' defence and security assessments. In general:

> when epistemic actors give advice, they often make value-laden and counterfactual judgments due to their normatively charged interpretative frames. When partisans disagree over free trade or arms control or foreign aid, the disagreements hinge on more than easily ascertained claims about trade deficits or missile counts or leaky transfer buckets. The disputes also hinge on hard-to-refute counterfactual claims about what would have happened if we had taken different policy paths and on impossible-to-refute moral claims about the types of people we should aspire to be – all claims that partisans can use to fortify their positions against falsification. (Tetlock 2005: 4)

The requirement of a separation between facts and values is hard to meet in the security field, and even more so when there is a pooling of expertise.

The security complex

'Failed states' and international terrorism require both civilian and military solutions. In line with requests from the Political and Security Committee, the EU has started to 'identify concrete actions to promote synergies between the EU civil and military capability development' (European Council 2010: 1). Security as a policy field has not only grown in importance, but has also broken new ground with regard to the requirement of new sorts of expertise. Security has become a multifaceted phenomenon which ranges from immediate security problems of regional conflicts, weak or failed states and organized crime to developmental aid to meet humanitarian needs. According to the comprehensive security concept there is a need for expertise that goes beyond traditional questions of defence, ranging from pertinent human rights issues via information and communication technologies to linguistic and regional, cultural and sociological expertise. Security expertise is, however, presently fragmented, discipline-bound and far from comprehensive. Partly this is owing to the fact that in a democratic state the tasks of the different internal and external security agencies are separated constitutionally, while 'advice depends on the pooling of expert advice from all fields involved in the management of a particular security problem' (Schröder 2006: 486).

Interlinked security challenges require interlinked knowledge about facts and causal connections. There is a wider role for a more complex bulk of knowledge; and not only of more facts. Fact-finding missions should be complemented with normative analyses, as issues need to be sorted out in relation to what problems they raise with regard to the rule of law, accountability and the legal protection of individual rights. Human rights, dignity-protecting rights, should not be treated on a par with pragmatic concerns for industrial and political effectiveness according to the principles of the constitutional state. Striking the right balance between political gains and personal freedom, between security and rights' protection, requires balancing according to qualitatively different metrics. Some of these dilemmas go to the heart of basic rights, while others raise merely pragmatic concerns as to what is the most rational means to build security and stability. One may fear that pragmatic concerns dominate. The Commission-issued communiqué of February 2004, in which a broader agenda of establishing a separate security research programme to facilitate an EU *security culture* was suggested, is telling:

> Europe needs to invest in a 'security culture' that harnesses the combined and relatively untapped strengths of the 'security' industry and the research community in order to effectively and innovatively address existing and future challenges. (European Commission 2004: 2)

The concept of deliberative democracy is particularly well suited for handling such questions, as it is premised on the presumption that only a reasoned debate taking all points of view into consideration, including normative ones, yields a viable outcome. However, in the EU, the 'pillarization' of the security field, the compartmentalization of expert knowledge, and the general convolution and opacity of the decision-making system make a sound process of expert advice and democratic accountability difficult to obtain.

The obsolescence of hierarchical accountability

The complexity of this policy area and the many bodies of knowledge called upon makes it difficult to ensure the necessary boundaries between the branches of government in general. This is even more so in the EU, where the security agenda is divided between the portfolios of the Commission and the Council; between the community method and the intergovernmental method. The co-operation between both the Terrorism Working Group (TWG) – (former) third pillar – and the Working Group on Counter-Terrorism (COTER)[5] – (former) second pillar – is in this case illustrative. Although the COTER deals with threats from third countries and TWG with law enforcement, merging both structures has been suggested owing to 'co-ordination problems' (European Council 2002, 2004).

The entry into force of the Lisbon Treaty (2009) implied a partial abolition of the pillar structure;[6] the establishment of a High Representative of the Union for Foreign Affairs and Security Policy (Article 18 TEU) and of the European External Action Service (EEAS). The High Representative holds a double-hatted post as President of the Foreign Affairs Council and Vice-President of the Commission. In reality, however, the post is *triple-hatted* in the sense that it covers the tasks which were attributed by the former Treaties to three bodies: the High Representative; the Commissioner for External Affairs; and the President of the External Relations Council. Hence, the authority and accountability lines are complicated. Moreover, processes of institution-building catch on as more competences are assigned with rising demand for knowledge. This is also the case with the CSDP.

The EU, in this field, formally relies on the three major professional communities: in-house expertise; advice of professional security services and defence industry interest representation; plus national foreign and defence ministries. For example, with regard to EU security, in-house expertise and advice to EU policy-makers are provided by the Council's Joint Situation Centre (SitCen) and Policy Unit of the High Representative, as well as from the professional security services such as the EU's Military Staff and different Council working groups staffed with national police and intelligence experts.[7] The SitCen, which is situated at the EU General Secretariat, is a merger of internal and external dimensions of EU counter-terrorism policy; it analyses intelligence material and monitors crisis situations. Information from internal and external services is fused in order to improve the knowledge-base of decision-making at the European level. This helps bridge the gap between the second and third pillar of the EU and to stream-line internal and external security analysis capability. The military representatives of the European Union Military Committee and the Civilian Crisis Management Committee report to the Political and Security Committee, which is comprised of member states' ambassadors.[8] They are responsible for crisis management operations under CSDP (Davis Cross 2010; see also Stie 2008).

In the traditional state-based approach, accountability means control of decision-makers by linking them to 'the democratic chain of delegation'

(Bovens *et al.* 2010: 54). Accountability through delegation – through handing over competences to the Union, competences that can be revoked (cp. Pollack 2003) – is increasingly difficult owing to the autonomy and discretion of decision-making bodies. Systems of delegation suffer from agency drift, unclear zones of discretion and lack of transparency and accountability (Eriksen and Fossum 2011: 158). The problem in the EU is that even though CSDP is formally intergovernmental, in reality there is a move beyond (Sjursen 2011). However, there is also no clear Europeanization of competences. The field has a tricky in-between status, which makes accountability difficult. For example, the opposition to Europeanization of anti-terrorism politics has resulted in a 'complex and blurred transnational sphere of counterterrorism' (den Boer *et al.* 2008: 103–4).[9]

One may ask, however, whether the *governance approach* constitutes an alternative strategy for meeting the accountability requirement in this policy field, where the lines of authority are complex and where it is difficult to dis-tinguish facts and values, experts from non-experts. The comprehensive security concept heightens these problems as it fuses different knowledge bases and forms of expertise. The governance approach is interesting because it goes beyond the formal system of authorization and democratic control. It is empirically relevant as we indeed witness the formation of transgovernmental networks, coalitions and committees across the formal system.[10] There is an, up to now, novel breed of knowledge-based and networked form of expert advice provided by a number of new groups of actors existing alongside the entrenched triangle of advisory boards, interests groups and bureaucracies. A series of new external actors, including epistemic agents, have approached Brussels.[11] Moreover, the openness to lobbyists and national élites, to non-governmental organisations (NGOs) and interest groups, think-tanks and consultants that have mushroomed in Brussels – the multiple access points for the entry of specialist knowledge – make the EU stand out in marked contrast to the more structured, segmented and closed relationship between knowledge and political decision-making in modern states. As is demonstrated elsewhere in this collection, this is increasingly so also in the security field.[12] Even in this field, governance is on the agenda in the EU. It is seen as a consequence of 'the inadequacy of *national* solutions, but also of the increasing limitations, in a changing post-Cold War world, of traditional *Alliance* policies' (Webber *et al.* 2004: 18, emphasis original; cp. Krahmann 2003). Is there, then, a new mode of rule in sight – one that can be theorized and which can meet the requirement of democratic accountability?

Experimental inquiry

Governance in most definitions includes government but reaches beyond it as well. It entails downplaying the authority structure of government and upgrad-ing the network character of modern policy-making. Governance entails the proliferation of actors and stakeholders in policy-making beyond the formal, legal authorisation of political law-making and implementation. It depicts a variety of processes with different authority bases, and highlights the role of voluntary and non-profit organisations – of social partners, civil society organizations and citizens' movements – in joint decision-making and implementation, and thus the semi-public character of the modern political venture. Its putative democratic value stems from the openness to public debate and civil society involvement.

In line with this, some proponents of deliberative democracy claim that policy-making in committees and networks supplemented with civil society associations, international non-governmental organisations (INGOs), and social movements, have created transnational European communicative spaces. These, as well as other devices for democratic control and contestation – such as elections and a free press – can be seen as mechanisms of accountability and feedback that function to institutionalize fallibilism and an experimental attitude (cp. Rosenau 1997; Anderson 2006: 15). They represent functional equivalents to democracy. More contestation, disagreements and politicization of depoliticized matters may occur. Deliberation in spontaneous and horizontally dispersed polyarchies can shatter epistemes and interpretative frames; deter domination and dissolve false consensuses. This draws on the insight that the growth of democratic communication is a requirement for *experimental inquiry* – for pragmatic problem-solving – within most fields of action in modern societies (Dewey 1927).[13] Deliberation is an intelligent problem-solving method that can facilitate choice under conditions of risk.

Some argue that *the transnational governance structure* of the EU has made for the pooling of competences and knowledge to the degree that there is no basis for collective decisions other than an outcome that leaves all better, or at least as well off, as before.[14] The plurality of access points, disaggregation and deliberation in criss-crossing publics are seen as facilitating democracy in a multi-centred world of diverse, non-governmental actors. Deliberation so to speak substitutes state-based government. The latter is not needed because network is available and is an appropriate 'institutional expression of a dispersed capacity to engage in deliberation that helps determine the terms of discourse in the international system' (Dryzek 1999: 48). Networks are seen as the institutional software for reflexive deliberation.

An all-inclusive procedure?

Disregarding for a moment that lack of hierarchy, the formal institutions of democracy come at a cost: the comprehensive security concept of the EU based on the merging of different forms of expertise and network governance is appealing in a deliberative perspective. The participants have to justify their standpoints and decisions in an impartial manner in order to obtain agreement. When approximating the full reciprocity condition, deliberation raises the information level and contributes to rationality. Epistemic actors possess information that is not restricted to certain groups; and transgovernmental actors who have no formal authority to initiate, pass or strike down legislation work through informal mechanisms to shape agendas, mediate disputes and mobilize support. These actors possess a 'wealth of first-hand experience' that is of interest for policy-making bodies (Buchanan and Keohane 2006: 433–4).

The novel breed of science-based and networked form of expert knowledge may in fact be the right regime to establish a comprehensive security policy – that is, when operating under discursive constraints of impartiality and publicity. Science and networks establish the requisite knowledge base for a comprehensive security policy when subjected to the conversational constraints of a rational debate. That is when all viewpoints and facts are taken into consideration, when the integration and balancing of policy demands and the pooling of different knowledge bases are rationally scrutinized to such a degree that undue concerns and biased information and twisted framing are filtered out. If, for example, new security challenges, crisis management and intelligence concerns, as well as the issues of economic competitiveness of the defence industry, are included and weighted against quests for developmental aid to meet humanitarian needs, and are then brought together in a wide-ranging, criss-crossing discourse in which experts (including lawyers) and human rights activists take part, the requirements of a comprehensive security policy may be approximated. The deliberative approach, which allows for free access of all arguments and viewpoints, may in principle be able to establish the standards for the construction of a comprehensive security concept in an increasingly complex security environment.

Deliberation is a fact-finding as well as a justification device. However, not all affected can generally be heard; there is limited participation and not all decision-making premises can be openly and rationally scrutinized. The resources – competence, capacity and time – to smash dogmatic world views, to deter domination and separate value-judgements and counterfactuals from 'objective' defence and security assessments are in short supply. This is even more so under the present conditions. When terrorist threats prevail, when life and security are perceived as threatened, a broad scope for secrecy and discretion on the basis of cemented values appears justified. Secrecy is a way to control the definition of the situation. Often the principles for secrecy fail to be subjected to public scrutiny. The rules that the citizens are subjected to cannot possibly meet the requirement of being justified with mutually acceptable reasons. How, to strike the right balance with regard to the pertinent moral and ethical issues involved when *the institutional hardware for reflexive deliberation* is not in place? In some policy areas, upholding the formal structure of the constitutional state is more imperative than in others.

PART III: THE BLURRING OF BOUNDARIES

The problem of de-formalization

Lack of hierarchy comes at a price. When hard law is missing, principled issues related to the protection of the fundamental individual rights are easily glossed over. This is a real danger to which the growing structure of *security governance* testifies. In national responses to terrorism after 9/11, the principles of the *Rechtsstaat* are often undermined.[15] According to Rainer Nickel there is a need to understand national responses to terrorism after 9/11 in a wider context as 'they are embedded in a growing structure of security governance ... [which] has evolved into a Global Militant Security Governance' (Nickel 2010: 1). There is a new quality in transnational security co-operation: 'It is, firstly, a new quality of a de-formalisation of security governance processes. Facilitated by email and the Internet, security agencies and police authorities can exchange information much faster and easier than ever before, and without leaving a paper trace. ... Secondly, this exchange culture promotes the dissolution of institutional and legal boundaries between criminal investigators (police and prosecutors) and those "secret" government agencies whose sole task is to gather information, again for limited purposes' (Ibid: 16f). 'The war on terror' seems to create something like *a new global security regime*. The United Nations Security Council (UNSC) resolutions on terror[16] 'entail the direct impact of harsh rights-violating sanctions on individuals and legislative commands distinct from crisis management "measures" addressed to states' (Cohen 2010: 15).

The same blurring of institutional and legal boundaries is seen in the comprehensive security concept. The intention is to 'demilitarize' security policy, but the call for a multifaceted bulk of knowledge would in fact imply the crossing of the legal walls of the democratic *Rechtsstaat*. The problem with the merging of quite disparate forms of expertise including policy concerns and intelligence is that they raise different moral and legal concerns that call for different procedures to be handled correctly. For example, in the ongoing fight against terrorism we have seen that 'the need to share essential information to prevent terrorist attacks has at times led to a convergence of police and intelligence work in which the formerly separate areas of criminal investigation and intelligence provision have become blurred' (Schröder 2006: 486). In a broad 'cross-pillar' action, the EU has, in fact, made use of the entire range of powers at their disposal in the fight against terrorism (Husabø and Bruce 2009: 4).

Security governance raises both the *red-tape argument*, as the line between the powers becomes blurred, and *the firewall argument*, as the institutional boundaries are distorted. The merging of different forms of expertise may endanger the fundamental freedoms of individuals.[17] The fundamental rights, which protect the freedom, integrity and privacy of individuals and minorities and which are now under attack because of the new terrorist/security agenda, need the autonomy and hierarchy of courts and judicial review in order to prevail. Some rights are inalienable and non-disposable also according to constitutional statutes. *Jus cogens* norms – non-derogable norms – are superior to both customary international law and treaty law. Ensuring dignity-protecting rights is difficult without the institutionalized division of labour between legislative, executive and judicial branches of power. This directs us to some of the principal limitations of the governance approach.

Deliberation plus

While deliberative governance allows for an unrestrained space of reasons so that everything can be taken into consideration, it cannot tell what is valid as it contains no standards for rational adjudication or prioritisation. What to do when not all can participate, when there is no consensus? Which reasons should rank higher in the final judgement? In a modern state, the people do not rule directly but exercise sovereignty and power through specific legislative, judicial and executive bodies. The principle of legality and the separation of powers ensure the democratic programming of administration – and not the self-programming of experts or special interests – and bar against executive dominance and the self-acquisition of power by bureaucratic bodies.

The requirements of deliberative accountability cannot be met without formal procedures of law-making and implementation in place, allowing the citizens to ask pertinent questions and effectively determine whether the answers provided are good enough. When not all can participate, when consensuses cannot be reached, criteria for how to decide on a range of questions are needed. It must be established who are really affected, whom to consult, how to represent, who should be held to account and how to sanction non-compliance, and so on. In short, when not all can participate and have a say, when conflicts thrive with or without good reason, one needs agreed-upon criteria of representation, decision-making and control, as well as of secrecy. Democratic accountability requires that the assignment of subjective rights is specified with regard to the explicit duties of the power-wielding bodies. The EU is, as mentioned, presently underdeveloped with regard to a clear structure of the separation of powers, contributing to 'a distancing between citizens, Union institutions and processes' (Conway 2011: 306; cp. Somek 2010). This is a field in which means and ends are hard to separate, where facts are infused with values, where it is hard to pinpoint an exact and specific knowledge base.

Problem-solving through governance structures should therefore be reserved for *low politics*: for pragmatic concerns, for technical and special issues. These, in principle, require 'merely' knowledge about facts and preferences in order to be solved properly, and as such do not raise moral or ethical questions of a politically salient nature. Foreign and security policy is not a special issue question, which experts or a particular group can resolve, but a common issue question. It is a salient political question that refers to the community *in toto*; it affects all to the same amount and degree. This policy-field refers to the nature and existence of the very polity – with the protection of the territory and the citizenry, to identity and border questions – which are of equal concern and interest for everyone. They cannot be left to experts or depoliticized decision-making bodies. Foreign and security policy is *high politics* and hence requires the institutional hardware for reflexive deliberation.

The upshot is that problem-solving in policy networks, which is endowed with discretionary power and no proper institutionalisation of accountability lines, cannot ensure rights' protection and rule out the dangers of *epistocracy and executive dominance* even under conditions of openness and publicity. Moreover, the call for expertise by EU actors may be seen as legitimation strategy, as a way to establish warrants and mobilize support, as there is no such thing as security expertise in a scientific sense of the word. In general, who is 'called an expert may have little to do with the possession of real and substantive' knowledge (Collins and Evans 2007: 2), and this is even more so in the security field.

CONCLUSION

From a democratic perspective, governance is conditional upon government as it is only in the 'shadow' of the law that governance bodies can legitimately operate. The complex and interlinked series of security threats, which are now spurred by the global financial crisis, call for comprehensive and concerted action in Europe. Given the fact that there is an increasing demand for scientific expertise in the field of security policy, one may ask whether this indisputably is a good thing. Science can only document facts, clarify normative concerns and establish means–end relations – it cannot act. When the epistemic inputs of experts are not democratically controlled, there is the danger of epistocracy.

With regard to the comprehensive security concept, which is the EU's brand nowadays, there are built-in, inextricable conflicts. They raise different normative concerns and pertain to different procedures and rights clauses. They must be handled by different decision-making bodies, specialized on explicit duties, in order to comply with the accountability requirement. Moreover, the whole talk of scientific expertise is seductive in this field so infused with values, where there hardly are hard facts and neutral knowledge. This talk may very well cover up for particular political motives.

The fact that the EU is presently underdeveloped with regard to the separation of powers and the general convolution and opacity of its decision-making system make democratic accountability difficult to obtain. The governance approach premised on deliberation cannot alleviate the democratic problem. Deliberation brings forth the utter fact of diversity and improves the quality of scientific advice, which is necessary in an increasingly complex security environment, but it cannot bear the burden of democratic legitimation.

Biographical note: Erik Oddvar Eriksen is Professor of Political Science and Director of ARENA – Centre for European Studies at the University of Oslo, and Scientific Coordinator of the FP6-funded project RECON – Reconstituting Democracy in Europe (http://www.reconproject.eu).

ACKNOWLEDGEMENTS

I am grateful for comments from Helene Sjursen, from three reviewers, and for help from ARENA's research assistants.

NOTES

1 The Butler Report, Review of Intelligence on Weapons of Mass Destruction, London, 14 July 2004, p. 138.
2 The Commission itself pointed to the need for ensuring rights in its 'White Paper on European governance' (European Commission 2001).
3 In these processes, the European Commission was accused of intransparency, vested interests and biased scientific advice, maladministration and lack of independence of scientific committees (Fischer 2008: 3).
4 See 'The European Security Research and Innovation Forum (ESRIF) – public–private dialogue in security research', *MEMO/07/346*, Brussels, 11 September 2007.
5 This is one of the two Council working parties which are entirely focused on the fight against terrorism. This situation remains unaltered after the Lisbon Treaty. The TWG handles practical co-operation (law enforcement), internal threat analysis and co-ordination between EU bodies. COTER deals with the external aspects of terrorism. See http://police-eu2010.be/mu-eu2010/en/working-groups/working-party-on-terrorism/ (accessed 15 June 2011).
6 Meaning the structure of three categories of co-operation with different areas of competence: the Economic Community (Pillar I); the Common Foreign and Security Policy (Pillar II); and Police and Judicial Co-operation in Criminal Matters (which are outside of Community law) (Pillar III). Following the introduction of a single legal personality (Art. 47 TEU), the third pillar will disappear after a transition period of five years (Protocol on Transitional Provisions, Art. 10). Policies in the field of justice and home affairs, including Schengen, will then be integrated into the first pillar. The partial abolition of the pillar structure is further evidenced by Art. 289 TFEU referring to the 'ordinary legislative procedure', which is specified in Art. 294 TFEU, and Art. 16 TEU on qualified majority. However CFSP/ESDP remains intergovernmental.
7 On the EU's military staff, see http://www.consilium.europa.eu/showPage.aspx?id=1039&lang=en (accessed 15 June 2011).
8 European Council (2001), see also the Council press release 'Preparatory document related to the CESDP: establishment of a European Committee for Civilian Crisis Management', 6755/00, 10 March 2000.
9 For example the Terrorism Working Party includes representatives from police forces and of the intelligence services of the member states as well as officials from the ministries in charge of combating terrorism (European Council 2004, 2009, 2011).
10 As Keohane and Nye (1974) observed: transgovernmental co-operation depicts the process under which sub-units of governments engage in direct and autonomous interaction separate from nation states.
11 The network which was initiated by the Commission on Radicalization (ENER) has grown into a dialogue between academics and policy makers working in the field (European Commission 2010). See also http://www.ec-ener.eu (accessed 15 June 2011).
12 See Joachim and Dembinski (2011). In their review on the European Security Strategy, Erik Brattberg and Mark Rhinard (2011) highlight the co-operation of the Commission with experts through seminars hosted by the European Union Institute for Security Studies (EUISS).

13 See Bohman (2007); see further Cohen and Sabel (1997, 2003); Gerstenberg (2002); Zeitlin and Trubek (2003); Sabel and Zeitlin (2010).
14 Marks *et al.* (1996); Joerges and Neyer (1997a, 1997b); Joerges and Vos (1999); Neyer (2003).
15 Cp. the lifting of the ban on torture in the Iraq war by the US.
16 UNSC Resolution 1267 in 1999 (concerning the Taliban); UNSC Resolution 1333 in 2000 (concerning Osama Bin Laden and Al Qaida); UNSC Resolution 1373 on 28 September 2001 (in the aftermath of 9/11); UNSC Resolution 1540 in 2004 (on weapons of mass destruction). Follow-up resolutions include UNSC Resolutions 1390 (concerning Afghanistan) and 1452 (on terrorist acts) in 2002 and UNSC Resolution 1483 in 2003 (on Iraq and Kuwait).
17 Basic constitutional rules – *jus cogens* norms – unconditionally protect the separation of powers, hence *the red-tape argument. The firewall argument* concerns human rights protection (see Eriksen 2006: 80).

REFERENCES

Anderson, E. (2006) 'The epistemology of democracy', *Episteme* 3(1–2): 8–22.
Beck, U. (1986) *Risikogesellschaft. Auf dem Weg in eine andere Moderne*, Frankfurt am Main: Suhrkamp.
Bigo, M. (2006) 'Global (in)security: the field and the ban-opticon', *Cultural Theory* 4: 109–57.
Bohman, J. (1996) *Public Deliberation. Pluralism, Complexity, and Democracy*, Cambridge, MA: MIT Press.
Bohman, J. (2007) *Democracy across Borders. From Dêmos to Dêmoi*, Cambridge, MA: MIT Press.
Bovens, M. (2007) 'Analysing and assessing accountability: a conceptual framework', *European Law Journal* 13(4): 447–68.
Bovens, M., Curtin, D. and Hart, P. (eds) (2010) *The Real World of EU Accountability. What Deficit?* Oxford: Oxford University Press.
Brattberg, E. and Rhinard, M. (2011) 'Reviewing the European Security Strategy', in *EEUUS Security Strategies: Comparative Scenarios and Recommendations*, Full Report, Pilot Project on Transatlantic Methods for Handling Global Challenges, pp. 27–36.
Buchanan, A. and Keohane, R.O. (2006) 'The legitimacy of global governance institutions', *Ethics and International Affairs* 20(4): 405–37.
Cohen, J.L. (2010) 'Constitutionalism beyond the state: myth or necessity?', *RECON Online Working Paper 2010/16*, Oslo: ARENA.
Cohen, J.L. and Sabel, C.F. (1997) 'Directly-deliberative polyarchy', *European Law Journal* 3(4): 313–42.
Cohen, J.L. and Sabel, C.F. (2003) 'Sovereignty and solidarity: EU and US', in J. Zeitlin and D.M. Trubek (eds), *Governing Work and Welfare in a New Economy*, Oxford: Oxford University Press, pp. 345–75.
Collins, H. and Evans, R. (eds) (2007) *Rethinking Expertise*, Chicago, IL: University of Chicago Press.
Conway, G. (2011) 'Recovering a separation of powers in the European Union', *European Law Journal* 17(2): 323–43.
Council of the European Union (2003) 'A secure Europe in a better world: European Security Strategy', Brussels, 12 December 2003.
Davis Cross, M.K. (2010) 'Cooperation by committee: the EU Military Committee and the Committee for Civilian Crisis Management', *EUISS Occasional Paper 82*, European Union Institute for Security Studies, available at http://www.iss.europa.eu/uploads/media/op82_CooperationbyCommittee.pdf (accessed 15 June 2011).

Dahrendorf, R. (1974) 'Citizenship and beyond: the dynamics of an idea', *Social Research* 41: 673–701.

den Boer, M., Hillebrand, C. and Nölke, A. (2008) 'Tightening the net around radicalization and recruitment: notes on the legitimacy of European counter-terrorism initiatives', in S. Virta (ed.), *Policing Meets New Challenges. Preventing Radicalization and Recruitment*, Tampere: Tampere University Press.

Dewey, J. (1927) *The Public and its Problems*, New York: Holt.

Dowdle, M.W. (2006) 'Public accountability: conceptual, historical, and epistemic mappings', in M.W. Dowdle (ed.), *Public Accountability. Designs, Dilemmas and Experiences*, Cambridge: Cambridge University Press, pp. 1–29.

Dryzek, J.S. (1999) 'Transnational democracy', *Journal of Political Philosophy* 7(1): 30–51.

Ellul, J. (1954) *The Technological Society*, New York: Vintage Books.

Elster, J. (2007) *Explaining Social Behavior. More Nuts and Bolts for the Social Sciences*, Cambridge: Cambridge University Press.

Eriksen, E.O. (2006) 'Democratic or jurist made law? On the claim to correctness', in A.J. Menéndez and E.O. Eriksen (eds), *Arguing Fundamental Rights*, Dordrecht: Springer, pp. 69–99.

Eriksen, E.O. (2009) *The Unfinished Democratization of Europe*, Oxford: Oxford University Press.

Eriksen, E.O. and Fossum, J.E. (2011) 'Bringing European democracy back in – or how to read the German Constitutional Court's Lisbon Treaty ruling', *European Law Journal* 17(2): 153–71.

European Commission (2001) 'European governance: a White Paper', *COM(2001) 428*, 25 July 2001, Brussels: European Commission.

European Commission (2002) *Science and Society Action Plan*, Luxembourg: Office for Official Publications of the European Communities.

European Commission (2004) 'Towards a programme to advance European security through research and technology', Communication on the implementation of the Preparatory Action on the enhancement of the European industrial potential in the field of Security research', *COM(2004) 72 final*, 3 February 2004, Brussels: European Commission.

European Commission (2010) 'The EU counter-terrorism policy: main achievements and future challenges', *COM(2010) 386*, 20 July 2010, Brussels: European Commission.

European Council (2002) 'Role and future working methods of the Working Group on Terrorism (COTER)', *11231/02*, 31 July 2002, Brussels: European Commission.

European Council (2004) 'Working structures of the Council in terrorism matters – options paper', *9791/04*, 25 May 2004, Brussels: Council of the European Union.

European Council (2009) 'European Security Research and Innovation Forum (ESRIF)', *8001/09*, 24 March 2009, Brussels: Council of the European Union.

European Council (2010) 'Promoting synergies between the EU civil and military capabilty – way ahead', *17285/10*, 6 December 2010, Brussels: Council of the European Union.

European Council (2011) 'Summary of discussions', *9429/11*, 27 April 2011, Brussels: Council of the European Union.

European Parliament (2011) 'EU counter-terrorism policy: main achievements and future challenges, draft report', *INI/2010/2311*, 29 March 2011.

Fischer, F. (2009) *Democracy and Expertise. Reorienting Policy Inquiry*, Oxford: Oxford University Press.

Fischer, R. (2008) 'European governance still technocratic? New modes of governance for food safety regulation in the European Union', *European Integration online Papers (EIoP)* 12(6), available at http://eiop.or.at/eiop/index.php/eiop/article/view/2008_006a

Gerstenberg, O. (2002) 'The new Europe: part of the problem: or part of the solution to the problem?' *Oxford Journal of Legal Studies* 22(3): 563–71.

Goodin, R.E. (2005) *Reflective Democracy*, Oxford: Oxford University Press.

Gross, E. (2008) 'EU and the comprehensive approach', *DIIS Report 2008:13*, Copenhagen: Danish Institute for International Studies.

Gutmann, A. and Thompson, D.F. (1996) *Democracy and Disagreement*, Cambridge, MA: Harvard University Press.

Habermas, J. (1969) *Technik und Wissenschaft als Ideologie*, Frankfurt am Main: Suhrkamp.

Habermas, J. (1996) *Between Facts and Norms. Contributions to a Discourse Theory of Law*, Cambridge, MA: MIT Press.

Harlow, C. (2002) *Accountability in the European Union*, Oxford: Oxford University Press.

Husabø, E.J. and Bruce, I. (2009) *Fighting Terrorism through Multilevel Criminal Legislation*, Leiden: Martinus Nijhoff.

Joachim, J. and Dembinski, M. (2011) 'A contradiction in terms? NGOs, democracy, and European Foreign and Security Policy', *Journal of European Public Policy* 18(8): 1155–68.

Joerges, C. and Neyer, J. (1997a) 'Transforming strategic interaction into deliberative problem-solving: European comitology in the foodstuffs sector', *Journal of European Public Policy* 4(4): 609–25.

Joerges, C. and Neyer, J. (1997b) 'From intergovernmental bargaining to deliberative political processes: the constitutionalisation of comitology', *European Law Journal* 3(3): 273–99.

Joerges, C. and Vos, E. (eds) (1999) *EU Committees. Social Regulation, Law and Politics*, Oxford: Hart.

Joerges, C., Ladeur, K.-H. and Vos, E. (eds) (1997) *Integrating Scientific Expertise into Regulatory Decision-Making. National Traditions and European Innovations*, Baden-Baden: Nomos.

Keohane, R.O. and Nye, J.S. (1974) 'Transgovernmental relations and international organizations', *World Politics* 27(1): 39–62.

Krahmann, E. (2003) 'Conceptualizing security governance', *Cooperation and Conflict* 38(1): 5–26.

Mansbridge, J. (2009) 'A "selection model" of political representation', *Journal of Political Philosophy* 17(4): 369–98.

Marks, G., Hooghe, L. and Blank, K. (1996) 'European integration from the 1980s: state-centric v. multi-level governance', *Journal of Common Market Studies* 34(3): 341–78.

Neyer, J. (2003) 'Discourse and order in the EU', *Journal of Common Market Studies* 41(4): 687–706.

Nickel, R. (2010) 'Data mining and "renegade" aircrafts: the states as agents of a global militant security governance network – the German example', *RECON Online Working Paper 2010/21*, Oslo: ARENA.

Pollack, M.A. (2003) *The Engines of European Integration. Delegation, Agency and Agenda Setting in the EU*, Oxford: Oxford University Press.

Rosenau, J.N. (1997) *Along the Domestic–Foreign Frontier. Exploring Governance in a Turbulent World*, Cambridge: Cambridge University Press.

Sabel, C. and Zeitlin, J. (eds) (2010) *Experimentalist Governance in the European Union*, Oxford: Oxford University Press.

Saint-Simon, H. (1975 [1760–1825]) *Henri Saint-Simon (1760–1825): Selected Writings on Science, Industry, and Social Organization*, trans. and ed. by K. Taylor, New York: Holmes and Meier Publishers.

Schelsky, H. (1961) *Der Mensch in der wissenschaftlichen Zivilisation*, Cologne: Westdeutscher Verlag.

Schröder, U.C. (2006) 'Security expertise in the European Union: the challenges of comprehensiveness and accountability', *European Security* 15(4): 471–90.

Sjursen, H. (2011), 'Not so Intergovernmental after all? On democracy and integration in European Foreign and Security Policy', *Journal of European Public Policy* 18(8): 1078–95.

Somek, A. (2010) 'The argument from transnational effects II: establishing transnational democracy', *European Law Journal* 16(4): 375–94.

Stie, A.E. (2008) 'Decision-making void of democratic qualities? An evaluation of the EU's foreign and security policy', *RECON Online Working Paper 2008/20*, Oslo: ARENA.

Tetlock, P.E. (2005) *Expert Political Judgment: How Good Is It? How Can We Know?* Princeton, NJ: Princeton University Press.

Webber, M., Croft, S., Howorth, J., Terriff, T. and Krahmann, E. (2004) 'The governance of European security', *Review of International Studies* 30(1): 3–26.

Weber, M. (1921 [1978]) *Economy and Society. An Outline of Interpretative Sociology*, Berkeley, CA: University of California Press.

Zeitlin, J. and Trubek, D.M. (eds) (2003) *Governing Work and Welfare in a New Economy*, Oxford: Oxford University Press.

Democratic foundations of EU foreign policy: narratives and the myth of EU exceptionalism

Ben Tonra

ABSTRACT How can we better understand weaknesses in the democratic legitimacy underpinning European Union (EU) foreign, security and defence policy? The argument presented here is that this weakness can in part be seen as a function of poor narrative construction in Europe. The nascent European public space does not yet provide a solid foundation from which such narratives might be established, contested and developed and from which they might aspire to some hegemony. Instead, the Union remains reliant upon an unstable intersection of national foreign policy narratives and the weak instantiation of an élite European narrative based on exceptionalism. This fails to create a sense of ownership and legitimacy over the international actions of the Union, adversely impacting its effectiveness and credibility. The élite narrative has solid roots in policy, academic and specialist constituencies but is weakly disseminated and vigorously contested.

INTRODUCTION

We are familiar with the basic premise: the Union is developing its capacity as a political actor and this must be made democratically legitimate. Two options are available. The first argues that the European Union's (EU) legitimacy is a function of its member states and it must operate according to a (modified) form of intergovernmentalism. This entails consensus decision-making, veto rights, respect for national sovereignty and policy-making through a system of complex interstate bargaining. The second argues that because the Union's legitimacy is grounded in its own nature as a political community, supranational or multi-level forms of governance are also required. This entails creating substantive democratic links between the Union and 'citizens' to offset majoritarian decision-making and policy-making among the member states.

In the realm of foreign, security and defence policy, we have an ideal-type case study grounded in the first model: where intergovernmentalism rules. What, then, are the consequences as member state governments work towards the creation of a 'common' policy, but eschew the traditional means by which such policies have been legitimated within the EU? Is there even a problem at all? It might be assumed that so long as the core veto rules apply, then member state governments are already held accountable by their electorates.

Legitimating this area of intergovernmental co-operation is seen as problematic for at least two reasons. The first is that this policy area is already a place apart. Different rules apply at national level that have the effect of insulating foreign and security policy from public opinion. These often include restricted access to information, limitations on parliamentary oversight, and the invocation of national security as a buttress against scrutiny (Tonra 2009). When this is extrapolated in the construction and execution of a common EU policy, a problem of double-insulation arises. In a national setting this is offset by the sense that foreign, security and defence policy is 'above' normal politics, that party political gaming stops at the border and that, therefore, the projection of the state overseas is rooted in some broader consensus of national identity and the national interests that derive therefrom. This countervailing feature is absent in an EU context.

The second issue is that the sheer depth and intensity of member state interactions is potentially changing the nature of the game and having transformative effects over national policy. This derives from the creation of intensely integrated structures for policy development and policy execution. These generate a deeply instantiated set of collective norms of behaviour which have the effect of transforming national policy in ways which are not immediately evident within domestic political structures and which are not explicitly acknowledged or sanctioned. As national policy and policy actors are 'Europeanized' (Torreblanca 2001; Tonra 2001; Stavridis 2003; Wong 2006; Pomorska 2007; Lee-Ohlsson 2009) or 'Brusselized' (Allen 1998; Müller-Brandeck-Bocquet 2002; Breuer 2010), citizens may lose their purchase over that which is done in their name.

Again, does this necessarily give rise to a problem? Over time member states, and in some cases their electorates, have taken decisions both to extend and to deepen the 'ever closer union' upon which they have embarked. This is not a permissive consensus but a repeated, conscious and active sanction. Where such sanction has been sought and denied, as in the case of Denmark, opt-outs are available. Where such sanction has been sought and contested, as in the case of Ireland, clarification is provided. In such circumstances, are citizens any more alienated from EU foreign policy than they are from their own national policies? Moreover, although national policy may have been transformed, member states still retain the core right of veto. In addition, domestic political systems – and the European political system as a whole – remains wide open to political actors who would wish to reverse, reshape or to qualify their European engagement.

This, therefore, is the research question to which this contribution is addressed: how can we better understand perceived weaknesses in the democratic legitimacy underpinning EU foreign, security and defence policy? The argument to be presented here is that weaknesses in the democratic legitimacy of this policy area can at least in part be seen as a function of poor narrative construction. The nascent European public space does not yet provide a solid foundation from which such narratives might be established, contested and developed and from which they might aspire to some hegemony. Instead, the Union remains reliant upon an unstable intersection of national foreign policy narratives and the weak instantiation of an élite European narrative based on exceptionalism. The former narratives, linked to notions of national identity, are themselves frequently contested and provide a fragile base from which to act and from which to generate public engagement at European level. They also fail to create a sense of ownership and legitimacy over the international actions of the Union. The élite narrative has solid roots in policy, academic and specialist constituencies but is weakly disseminated and vigorously contested.

Developing arguments presented on national foreign policy (Tonra 2007), this contribution begins by recalling debates on foreign policy and identity and the ways in which state identity is produced, reproduced and challenged. This establishes a baseline analysis that argues that national foreign policies are existentially rooted in identity politics. The boundary-producing role of foreign policy is then explored in some detail as one of the social practices that assist in the definition of national identity and which is a marker of that identity's development and change. The contribution then assesses the extent to which such an analysis can be applied to the EU. Does the Union's international activity create boundaries and identities which are analogous to those created within states? This question is assessed so as to make an argument that the Union's foreign and security policy does play a comparable role in identity formation, but that there are significant differences which problematize its capacity to legitimate that policy. The argument offered here is that the EU's identity as a foreign policy actor is at least in part a function of contested national narratives, that the Union suffers from a weakly instantiated sense of self and that its fragile democratic legitimation is a partial outcome of that weakness. The essay will conclude by offering some comments on the implications of that weakness for the democratic legitimacy of the Union's foreign policy and where one might look for redress.

EUROPEAN FOREIGN POLICY AND IDENTITY

David Campbell (1992) has offered two conceptions of foreign policy. The first is that of foreign policy being the external representation of a state. The second is as 'one of the boundary-producing practices central to the production and reproduction of the identity in whose name it operates' (Campbell 1992: 75) Thus, foreign policy is itself defined as a discursive practice from which a collective social identity emerges. As a result, foreign policy has a crucial role in creating, reinforcing and challenging that identity just as it then proceeds to represent that identity externally (Campbell 1992; Waever 2002; Aggestam 2004). This defines the relationship between identity and foreign policy as being mutually constitutive and is illustrated by the statement of one European foreign minister; 'The elaboration of our foreign policy is also a matter of self-definition – simply put, it is for many of us a statement of the kind of people that we are' (cited in Tonra 2007: 2).

Identity is conceptualized here as being comprised of intersubjectively held understandings of group attributes and identifiers which are then defined through an ongoing process of discursive contestation (Abdelal *et al.* 2005). Benedict Anderson (1991) also looks at identity as an ongoing, contested process. This approach looks at a specified group of people and analyses their sharing of an 'imagined community'. His focus is very much upon the state of 'being' and the ongoing process of reproduction and identity change (Ullock 1996; Friis 2000).

Identity is constructed discursively, by way of language and other communicative systems – the 'processes and practices by which people and groups construct their self-image' (McSweeney 1996: 82). It is through the production and reproduction of these processes and practices that the notion of an identity is created, maintained and challenged. Identity becomes a reality as it is instantiated through the discourses of a variety of actors; politicians, journalists, community leaders, writers, educators, artists, activists, religious leaders, intellectuals and engaged citizens. It is disseminated through public and private communication within discursive spaces (Laclau and Mouffe 1985).

The discursive construction of identity is necessarily a political project that creates difference. Bill McSweeney's (1996) 'self-image' is also a creature of what it is not. Social identity theory has underlined the extent to which the definition of identity boundaries is a goal in itself – the boundaries do not so much provide a definition of the group's cultural content (of its history, language, etc.) but rather of the identity border which is itself intrinsically valuable. This opens up an analysis as to how and when those signifiers of belonging might change over time (Hansen 2005). Their evolution can now become more easily an object of study and the focus of this study is thus upon one set of these border markers – those denoting foreign policy.

It is important to emphasize again that identity is seen here as being neither immutable nor a zero-sum construction of self versus others – quite the contrary. The assumption of this study is that such intersubjective understandings underpinning identity can be re-imagined (Anderson 1991) and, through foreign policy, may be the subject of constant reproduction and evolution at home and abroad (Catalinac 2007: 74–5). That contestation may also be rooted in power relations with competing conceptions of identity present, either at the margins of political discourse or battling head-on for discursive supremacy. It is precisely this political, diplomatic and intellectual ferment which allows for identity change and, hence, in the shape, definition and objectives of foreign policy (Hopf 2002: 184).

For their part, narratives have the capacity to shape our understanding of the world. According to Lewis P. Hinchman and Sandra K. Hinchman (1997: xiv), they illustrate 'the power of stories to create and refashion personal identity'.

They also offer an integrated account of what might otherwise be seen as unconnected facts and events. Narratives often also simplify complex, conditional and excessively contextualized stories. In sum, narratives are the articulation of identity that is derived from discourse.

Narratives are also relational. In the first case, the success of a narrative rests on its ability to tell a better (and apparently more 'truthful') story than other competing narratives all of which are battling for discursive dominance. Secondly, narrative success is based upon its repeated iteration (constitution and reconstitution) over time through discursive processes (including foreign policy, as per Campbell above). Thus, the argument presented here is that in each of the Union's member states, there exists an ongoing narrative contestation underpinning that state, its foreign policy and national identity. In many cases, that identity and its associated narrative(s) may be deeply rooted with little or no apparent change over time. In other cases the contest between competing narratives for discursive dominance may be highly charged and very visible.

Even if a mutually constitutive relationship can reasonably be established between national identity and foreign policy in principle, is such a construction appropriate to the European Union? As we recall, Campbell first asserts that foreign policy is the external representation of a state. Certainly the Union is actively engaged in the external representation of itself and its member states collectively. Moreover, following the ratification of the Lisbon Treaty, the Union is seeking to represent itself in ways that are increasingly state-like. With the development of the Union's military capacity, the award of legal personality, its pursuit of speaking rights at the United Nations (UN), the creation of the External Action Service and the expanded role of the High Representative, the trajectory of the Union's development appears to be towards a modified model of a Westphalian state. It is also doing so not as a supernumerary member of the Union but as a vehicle through which the member states vest their collective interests and shared ambitions.

Campbell's second understanding of foreign policy is that it is 'one of the boundary-producing practices central to the production and reproduction of the identity in whose name it operates' (Campbell 1992: 75). Is EU foreign policy a discursive practice from which the Union's collective social identity emerges? To what extent does its practice create and instantiate identity boundaries? Certainly, in its creation and development we can trace a clear line of identity politics within EU foreign policy.

The mandate given to European foreign ministers at the 1969 Hague Summit was explicit. They were tasked with studying 'the best way of achieving progress in the matter of political unification, within the context of enlargement' (Hague Summit 1969: 16). When the ministers submitted their final proposals for the consideration of the heads of state and government on 27 October 1970 they recalled that precise instruction. As a consequence:

> [they] therefore felt that foreign policy concertation should be the object of the
> first practical endeavours to demonstrate to all that Europe has a political

vocation. The Ministers are, in fact, convinced that progress here would be cal-culated to promote the development of the Communities and give Europeans a keener awareness of their common responsibility. (Davignon 1970: 10)

The very *raison d'être* of foreign policy co-operation was thus to assist in the construction of a visible European identity. This was reasserted in the creation of the Common Foreign and Security Policy when, in 1990, Chancellor Helmut Kohl and President Francois Mitterand jointly wrote to the European Council Presidency setting out their shared goal of creating a 'European Union' and identifying closer foreign policy co-ordination as a critical element in estab-lishing that union. Moreover, this is no historic relict but is evident even in con-temporary policy execution. Christopher Bickerton notes that one of the core three functions of EU foreign policy is to assert its international identity and capacity where 'the *purpose* of ESDP seems to be the affirmation of the EU as an actor, with the policy action itself – e.g., a police or military mission — the *means* to that end' (Bickerton 2010: 222). Moreover, efforts to instantiate a European 'voice' and to personalize EU foreign policy in the creation and strengthening of the post of the High Representative, illustrate further the underpinning logic of the identification of EU foreign policy.

A preliminary stumbling block, to explicating the link between EU foreign policy and a collective identity is that the borders of the Union remain at issue. By definition, a foreign policy that has to encompass the possibility of enlargement to include new states, has to be diffident about striking hard and fast definitions of the 'other'. The possibility of the 'other' becoming part of the 'we' has to remain open. In addition, even those borders that do exist are pro-blematic. The Union's policy spaces are not coterminous. The borders of the Union's monetary union are not the same as the borders of its customs union and the borders of neither are the same as the borders of the Schengen zone of free movement. Furthermore, the Union's export of its policies to non-member states, through the European Economic Area (EEA) or the European Neighbourhood Policy (ENP) creates a 'fuzziness' over definitive delineations of who is in or who is out (Christiansen *et al.* 2000; Kux and Sverdrup 2000).

This has not, however, forestalled some substantial 'othering' through EU foreign policy. In the absence of hard and fast spatial borders, some have instead relied upon temporal boundaries. The Union is juxtaposed against Europe's past of war, genocide, dictatorship and unbridled nationalism (Waever 1998; Risse 2001; Diez 2004). The Union's very existence as an actor in the international system is then presented as being emblematic of success in overcoming history, holding lessons for others. Europe therefore pursues a 'new' kind of international politics. This is certainly evident through-out the practice of the Union's foreign policy; the demand for human rights clauses in its trade agreements, its acutely self-conscious pursuit of specified norms within multilateral institutions and international law, and its avowed commitment to the pursuit of sustainable development, justice and inter-national security.

In a perhaps more traditional vein, Union foreign policy also serves to underline a contradistinction with other international actors and with other identity narratives (Meinhoff 2004). The Union has been explicit, for example, in defending its socio-economic identity (the 'social market economy', and the European social model) as being profoundly different (and normatively superior) to that of the United States and of Japan. In some quarters, this is further extended to the political realm wherein Europe's defence of human rights, international law and multilateral institutions is used as a marker to distinguish Europe from the United States (US) (Diez 2005; Scheipers and Sicurelli 2007). In its ultimate expression, European foreign policy is presented as the drive train of a Europe conceived as a 'difference engine', challenging the entire Westphalian world order (Manners and Whitman 2003). Finally, the Union's foreign policy, through its justice, trade, aid, security and so-called 'neighbourhood' policies, underscores a tendency to define a European heartland in contrast to constructed models of a potentially threatening 'east' and/or 'south' (Neumann 1999; Whitman 2010).

If it is reasonable to conclude that the practice of the Union's foreign policy creates and instantiates boundaries, does it also produce and reproduce European identity? It is here that the symmetry between national and European foreign policy/identity relationships arguably breaks down – with critical implications for the democratic legitimacy of EU foreign policy.

EXCEPTIONALISM AND NARRATIVE ENGAGEMENT

The central empirical argument presented here is that EU foreign and security policy is constructed on a weak identity foundation and that this is evident across several dimensions; the construction of an inadequately instantiated narrative of European 'exceptionalism', the lack of substantive engagement between national foreign policy narratives and the absence of a European public sphere capable of either weaving national narrative elements into a coherent European whole or legitimating EU policy actions in any new narrative construction.

The context within which dominant and/or hegemonic national foreign policy narratives intersect is unique, even in European terms. As has been stated earlier, foreign policy decision-making is set apart from normal European policy models. Decision-making is firmly intergovernmental and consensual and it is from this formal and tightly delimited socio-political space that EU foreign and security policy is ultimately made. It would be wrong to argue, however, that the resulting EU policy nestles in the shadow of a reductionist mélange of national narratives. Instead, what appears to have been created, perched uncomfortably atop a set of diverse national foreign policy narratives, has been a well defined and vigorously promoted élite EU narrative based upon exceptionalism.

Exceptionalism has a chequered history in the study of foreign policy. More often than not, it is rooted in normative preferences as to national mission and purpose, i.e. that this state or that empire is acting differently, more correctly, more ethically or more appropriately than have earlier foreign policy actors or competing foreign policy actors (Lawler 1997; Vale and Taylor 1999; Lazarus

2004). In some rare instances, a case is made that this exceptionalism is based upon a profoundly different world view, resulting in a challenge to the way in which international relations (or indeed domestic politics) is conducted. The most obvious example here is that of the United States, where exceptionalism remains a powerful political credo (Lipsett 1996; Koh 2003).

Contemporary European exceptionalism is arguably no less challenging. Based on a temporal 'othering' of its history, the Union's founding narrative is of an historic reconciliation, a recognition of the dangers of unfettered nationalism and the creation of a new kind of polity as a European peace project (Beck and Grande 2007). Well-established tropes such as that of the Union being a *sui generis* creation, incomparable with other polities, offers a key starting point within academic debates. Limitations on the Union's early international profile; the absence of military capacity and its reliance upon trade and economic tools to sustain hard power, were also repackaged as creating a new kind of 'civilian' actor, exemplifying a new, liberal, interdependent age (Duchêne 1972).

However, as the Union has accreted additional international capacity, the associated narrative(s) have struggled to maintain their differentiation of the Union as an actor. The attempts are well catalogued; the Union as a 'difference engine' (Manners and Whitman 2003); a 'normative power' (Manners 2002); an 'ethical power' (Aggestam 2008); a 'postmodern' power (Kagan 2002; Cooper 2004); or even a 'civilian power' wielding military power in a civilian way (Bachmann and Sidaway 2009). At its core, however, a narrative of European exceptionalism insists that by virtue of its very existence, made real by its declared ambition (if not by its actions), the Union challenges the deeply instantiated norms of the Westphalian international system (Scheipers and Sicurelli 2007). Moreover, it does so not on the basis of any Eurocentric *mission civilisatrice*, but upon that of universal human values.

Perhaps perversely, this narrative of exceptionalism makes few hard and fast empirical claims. A variety of studies have examined EU behaviour in different policy realms and found little or no evidence of exceptionalism, instead pointing to the Union as a quite traditional international actor, focused upon discernable and salient member state interests (Hyde Price 2006; Zimmerman 2007). Instead of countering with a range of their own empirical examples, advocates of exceptionalism have largely relied upon meta-arguments centred on the Union's origins as a peace project, its unique institutional and decision-making structures, its rhetorical ambitions and textual declarations and its overall status as an exemplar of a new kind of inter-state politics. Indeed, one of the key contemporary architects in defining the Union in these terms has insisted that his is a normative argument, establishing a base line as to what the Union 'should be doing in world politics' rather than describing what it actually does in world politics (Manners 2006: 168).

The dearth of empirical substance, however, only highlights again the power of the intellectual conceit upon which this narrative of exceptionalism is founded and which is echoed back from the highest political levels. It clearly benefits from the strength of its narrative entrepreneurs in academic, political and diplomatic circles. However, its weakness is arguably to be found in the fact of the narrative's poor grounding in, and its limited reflection of, national foreign policy narratives. This rests also at the roots of the poor legitimation of EU foreign and security policy.

In sum, sets of respectively hegemonic national foreign policy narratives are intersecting at European level and only a weakly instantiated European narrative of exceptionalism is being reflected back. National foreign policy narratives resonate powerfully with a wide variety of identity images: French *puissance*; Finnish 'peacekeeping superpower'; German *zivilmacht*; etc. These images emerge from a well-spring of domestic discourses centred on their self-definition as a people, lessons from their historical experience, their ethics, their ambitions and even their subjective fears. These are distilled and contested through dense national public spaces and emerge to define the range of the possible in national foreign policy.

Nothing of comparable power or depth is being created at European level. National threads are not woven into an image of a Europe to which Europeans might offer even a tentative affective connection. The empirical evidence suggests that engagement between the national and the European results in contestation of the European (Tonra 2007), adaptation to the European (Palosaari 2011) or convergence to a European norm (Wong 2005). This systemic integration, however, is not buttressed by a social integration which could offer a credible and coherent pan-European narrative (Grimm 1995, 2005) and upon which an effective foreign and security policy might be built. This failure to connect a dominant EU foreign policy narrative with those forged in the respective member states, is arguably a function of three interconnected elements: a limited European public space; the double-insulation of EU foreign and security policy; and a critical failure of EU-level policy to make hard policy choices.

First, it is widely agreed that 'the European polity does not require a demos that replaces a national with a European identity, but one in which national and European identities coexist and complement each other' (Risse 2004: 250). While a hegemonic 'supranational' European narrative is neither sought nor expected, what appears still to be missing is the political space from which national complementarities might be identified and then drawn together to ground a larger European narrative, side-by-side with its national analogues.

There has been considerable analysis of the linkages between discursive public spaces and the development of a European identity (Fossum and Schlesinger 2007). In earlier scholarship the absence of a European public space was noted and its development seen as a precondition of substantive democratic legitimacy within the European project. Europe lacked both the common cultural and linguistic infrastructure from which such a singular space might be constructed (Graham 1992; Grimm 1995; Schlesinger 1999) as well as the supranational media system necessary to its creation (Schlesinger 1997; Kevin 2004). Other scholars have since argued that that the ideal-type public space that was originally postulated simply set the bar too high and that discursive European conversations could be identified in discrete policy areas (Risse 2002, 2003; Van de Steeg 2002;

Diez Medrano 2003; Koopmans and Pfetsch 2003; Trenz 2004). Thus, the focus was upon how national discursive spaces were being Europeanized and/or how such spaces handled European issues (Semetko *et al.* 2000; Sifft *et al.* 2007).

In terms of foreign policy, Thomas Risse and Jana Katharina Grabowsky argue that 'European identity is particularly visible in debates on foreign and security policy' (2008:1) and they identify a variety of elements – centred upon notions of 'civilian power' – that are contributing to a European identity. Like Jürgen Habermas and Jacques Derrida (2006), they highlight the February 2003 European demonstrations against the war in Iraq as marking the moment that 'a European public sphere became visible' (Risse and Grabowsky 2008: 11). This is perhaps overstating the case. It should be noted that the actor that should have benefitted from such a foundational expression of a distinct public will was utterly incapable of action. The EU was instead thrown into crisis as it proved itself unable to respond with a collective policy position of any substance. In addition, the scope of narrative discourse in this emblematic instance was remarkably narrow, amounting to little more than a 'point by point alternative to the imperial foreign policy of the United States' without any specific 'European' perspective (Tully 2007). What this illustrates is not that a nascent European public space does not exist, but that it as yet fails to marshal reinforcing national narratives into coherent policy outputs.

The hollow shell of a social infrastructure necessary to the creation of such a European public space in foreign policy is present: the Brussels-based think tanks; the 'associations' of national foreign policy institutes; the transnational (usually EU-funded) research projects; academic 'networks' on European foreign policy; learned journals; and even daily newsletters on EU foreign policy developments all exist. At the same time, just as elections to the European Parliament remain 'second order' events compared to their national analogues, this social infrastructure underpinning EU foreign policy fails to engage even the most attentive national publics in a truly 'European' debate on foreign, security and defence policy. Even when 'Europe' figures within major international crises, as in Bosnia, in Rwanda, in Georgia and in North Africa it is, like as not, simply bracketed alongside the United Nations (UN), the North Atlantic Treaty Organization (NATO) and a generic 'international community' as an external agent of which more is expected than is ever delivered. The sense that this 'Europe' has an agency which is open to direction by a European public is simply absent.

Second, the 'self-reinforcing executive dominance' (RECON 2008) exemplified by the Common Foreign and Security Policy (CFSP) and the Common Security and Defence Policy (CSDP) helps us to understand this disconnect. As noted above, policy élites have assiduously developed narratives of European exceptionalism as if to underpin their own self understanding of the unique political project that they have undertaken. It is also perhaps a means of assuring themselves and their respective publics that as far as foreign policy is concerned, nothing really has changed; vetoes remain, consensus rules, and there is no scintilla of federalism or supranationalism evident. This is also reflective of their reluctance to engage with the language of interests at European level. Doubly insulated from respective publics, policy makers are thereby untethered from the need to sustain a Europe-wide legitimation of policy. Critically, therefore, they are willing and perhaps anxious, to ensure that the chimera of 'national interest' is maintained.

Thus, how can attentive publics be convinced that there exists an EU agency over which they have any modicum of control, when the discourse presented to them by policy makers is that nothing has really changed, national foreign policy is unchanged/unchallenged and that the 'European' exists only as yet another (inadequate) framework through which the national is pursued internationally? This is even further underscored by the self-consciously 'diplomatic' nature of the CFSP/CSDP's institutional and decision-making structures and the deliberate walls drawn up between those structures and the rest of the Union, most especially the Commission, the Parliament and the Court of Justice.

The third element which goes some way to offering an understanding of the disconnect between the national and the European is the lack of evident ambition underpinning European policy. The chasm, which separates the Union's rhetorical flourishes on human rights, sustainable development and international justice from its policy practice with respect to China, Russia, North Africa, the Middle East and thematic issues such as climate change, can hardly lend itself to reinforcing the Union's credibility in the eyes of its own mass public(s). To a large extent – rhetoric notwithstanding – EU foreign policy continues to rest within a largely unobjectionable cloud of low intensity, multilateral peace keeping and neighbourhood-building and makes no real demands of itself or of its citizens. As a result, it avoids the kinds of vibrant public debates and hard choices at European level that might sustain and define a more powerful European public space. This creates an image of Europe as an international social worker rather than as a global power.

A note of caution here is apposite. It should not be assumed that a more profoundly democratic integration of European foreign policy will result in a necessarily more progressive foreign and security policy rooted in 'dialogues of many existing civilizations, alternative modernities and cosmopolities' (Tully 2007: 81). One might recall that one explicit justification of the insulation of foreign and security policy at national level is precisely to shield the state from the excesses of political demagoguery. One might even go so far as to wonder aloud whether the double insulation of EU foreign policy is perhaps rooted in some foundational fear of Europe's own imperial history and an indispensable ambivalence towards the exercise of European power, wielded explicitly in the name of a potent and well rooted European narrative.

DEMOCRATIC LEGITIMATION AND FOREIGN POLICY IDENTITY

A core claim of this contribution is that a collective identity is necessary to the democratic legitimation of foreign policy. This is evidenced at the levels of principle, practice, and praxis. At the level of principle, neither a 'statist shortcut'

(Grimm 1995) through federalism nor a diplomatic detour through the underbrush of the Lisbon Treaty can give life to the institutions tasked with the development and execution of EU foreign policy. The sterile titling of the High Representative and the External Action Service are no more than emblematic of the fact that these constructions do not possess the divine breath of agency. They are clearly simulacra, absent the existential quality and substance of their national analogues and they represent the 'autonomisation of bureaucratised politics' (Habermas 1995: 304). Without any serious effort to weave national foreign policy narratives into a broader European cloth, without the public space in which to conduct such a debate, these institutions can generate no affective link with European publics. As a result, national policy-makers can only seek to maintain and extend the 'self-reinforcing executive dominance' if they are to sustain a system of collective policy development.

In practice too, a well-grounded European foreign policy identity is necessary to sustain the legitimation of that policy. One of the ongoing critiques of the Union's foreign and security policy is that its credibility, coherence and effectiveness is at best problematic (Everts 2002; Solana 2003). Third parties rarely glimpse a 'Europe' when they look at the Union. The successful efforts of the US administration to 'cherry-pick' among European states for support of their 2003 invasion of Iraq underscores this fact, while the mass mobilization of European publics in opposition to that intervention was only partially reflected among European governments and was invisible at EU level throughout that crisis. Absent a collective identity to give democratic substance, support and weight to a collective European foreign policy, the Union's pale efforts serve only to highlight the – admittedly dense – multilateral and intergovernmental nature of its foreign policy institutions and decision-making processes. Moreover, the potential fracture lines in collective EU policy map directly and powerfully onto 'national interests', which await little more than the leverage of third parties to prise the policy apart. Finally, the absence of a strong European narrative results in every crisis being 'nationalized' once refracted through the lens of national public spaces. Notwithstanding planning cells, military structures and crisis management procedures, for example, the 2011 evacuations of European citizens from Libya were conducted wholly through national prisms, with European publics comparing and contrasting the treatment of their nationals against that of other EU and non-EU member states alike.

In terms of praxis however, there is both further evidence of the critical need for a stronger European identity narrative to sustain democratic legitimation of foreign policy, but also the glimmers of a resolution. The understanding that foreign policy exemplifies something more than raw self interest is widely acknowledged among both practitioners and analysts. Certainly, while the narrative of EU exceptionalism is both narrowly based and lacking firm grounding within respective national foreign policy narratives, it clearly resonates within élite policy communities in Brussels and some national capitals. If there is credible substance to an argument that Europe is indeed different and that it has the potential to make a difference, then seeing that visibly instantiated within a

European public space can only strengthen such a narrative, giving it power and presence. What is therefore sought is the 'the intersubjectively shared context of possible understanding' (Habermas 1995: 305) executed through European public spaces.

The argument presented here is that without a strong European foreign policy narrative, reflective of its national analogues and resonating with respective European publics, the Union cannot sustain an effective or credible foreign policy. That is not to say that such a collective identity is an a priori precondition nor that such a collective identity can be created by the methods used in the construction of the Westphalian state. Instead, it suggests that in the construction of a common policy greater attention must be paid to social as well as systemic integration. Time, attention and resources must be devoted to filling the hollow shells of the social infrastructure identified above. Arguably, Europe missed its constitutional moment in 1948 with the formation of the Council of Europe. Perhaps, however, we need to remind ourselves of the genesis of European Political Co-operation as a means of giving political reality to European construction so that the Union is constructed both as forum for action but critically also as a mental space of reflection.

CONCLUSIONS

The European project is pushing at limits of what has traditionally been defined as a permissive consensus. The development of CFSP and CSDP exacerbates this, as foreign policy, security and defence are often seen as resting at the apex of the creation of a political community – representing the ultimate 'we' feeling. If the Union stands at a juncture of making demands of citizens in terms of peace and war – if it is truly setting out to define itself, its member states and citizens' place and role in the world, then this must be legitimated in ways not yet accomplished in European construction. Moreover, if such legitimation is unavailable through the formal structures of communitarian decision-making then informal channels of the type that operate at national level are all the more meaningful.

If it is reasonable to define the problem in the above terms, then we can plausibly look to the experience of member states in the legitimation of their foreign and security policies. As has been noted above, however, those parallels have limitations. Identity is reflected through foreign policy, and we can see this in the case of the European Union. At the same time, there is an appreciation that the Union 'will not be constructed in the fashion of the historic European nation, once humorously defined as a group of people united by a common hatred of their neighbours and a shared misunderstanding of their past' (Garton Ash 2007). The pursuit of a unifying European foreign policy narrative is also problematic; whether or not it relies upon 'othering' the US, Islam, the 'East' or indeed its own past.

There are significant myths of Europe's place in the world (Nicolaïdis and Howse 2002; Manners 2010) that might serve as underpinnings to such an endeavour. Such threads are visible in national foreign policy narratives across the European Union. This contribution suggests, however, that at present there is insufficient discursive heat within a European public space and the social infrastructure available is too fragile to forge ties between national and European narrative constructions. As Paul Gillespie and Brigid Laffan (2006) argue in the context of national identity, the concept of a European foreign policy identity has to be closely anchored in established concepts of national foreign policy identity.

The formality and insulation of foreign policy and decision-making at European level militates strongly against the substantive engagement of citizens with that policy, their reflection in that policy and their sense of ownership over that policy. This is perhaps not so acute a problem if the policy project was clearly delimited and precisely defined. However, political and diplomatic élites are arguably creating their own paradox by seeking to present a more coherent, effective and united face to the world while simultaneously seeking to use the construction of that face as a means towards creating a political community (Bickerton 2010). Democratic legitimacy is critical to both sides of this equation and it is arguably missing in both.

Biographical note: Ben Tonra is Jean Monnet Professor of European Foreign, Security and Defence Policy and Associate Professor of International Relations at the UCD School of Politics and International Relations.

REFERENCES

Abdelal, R., Herrera, Y.M., Johnston, A.I. and McDermott, R. (2005) 'Identity as a variable: measuring the content and contestation of a variable', Weatherhead Initiative in International Affairs, Harvard University.
Aggestam, L. (2004) 'A European Foreign Policy. Role conceptions and the politics of identity in Britain, France and Germany', *Stockholm Studies in Politics*, 106, Stockholm: Stockholm University.
Aggestam, L. (2008) 'Introduction: ethical power Europe?', *International Affairs* 84(1): 1–11.
Allen, D. (1998) 'Who speaks for Europe?', in J. Peterson and H. Sjursen (eds) *A Common Foreign Policy for Europe? Competing Visions for CFSP*, London and New York: Routledge, pp. 41–58.
Anderson, B. (1991) *Imagined Communities. Reflections on the Origin and Spread of Nationalism*, London: Verso.
Bachmann, V. and Sidaway, J.D. (2009) 'Zivilmacht Europa: a critical geopolitics of the European Union', *Transactions* 34(1): 94–109.
Beck, U. and Grande, E. (2007) *Cosmopolitan Europe*, Cambridge: Polity Press.
Bickerton, C. (2010) 'Functionality in EU foreign policy: towards a new research agenda', *Journal of European Integration* 32(2): 213–27.

Breuer, F. (2010) 'Between intergovernmentalism and socialisation: the Brusselisation of ESDP', *RSCAS Working Papers 48*, Florence: Robert Schuman Centre for Advanced Studies (RSCAS).

Campbell, D. (1992) *Writing Security. United States Foreign Policy and the Politics of Identity*, Minneapolis, MN: University of Minnesota Press.

Catalinac, A. (2007) 'Identity theory and foreign policy: explaining Japan's responses to the 1991 Gulf War and the 2003 US war in Iraq', *Politics and Policy* 35(1): 58–100.

Christiansen, T., Petito, F. and Tonra, B. (2000) 'Fuzzy politics around fuzzy borders: the European Union's near abroad', *Cooperation and Conflict* 4(35): 389–415.

Cooper, R. (2004) *The Breaking of Nations. Order and Chaos in the Twenty-First Century*, London: Atlantic.

Davignon, E. (1970) 'Report by the foreign ministers of the member states on the problems of political unification', *Bulletin of the European Communities*, 11 November: 9–14.

Diez, T. (2004) 'Europe's others and the return of geopolitics', *Cambridge Review of International Affairs* 17(2): 319–35.

Diez, T. (2005) 'Constructing the self and changing others: reconsidering "normative power Europe"', *Millennium: Journal of International Studies* 33(3): 613–36.

Diez Medrano, J. (2003) *Framing Europe. Attitudes to European Integration in Germany, Spain and the United Kingdom*, Princeton, NJ: Princeton University Press.

Duchêne, F. (1972) 'Europe's role in world peace', in R. Mayne (ed.), *Europe Tomorrow. Sixteen Europeans Look Ahead*, London: Fontana, pp. 32–47.

Everts, S. (2002) *Shaping a Credible EU Foreign Policy*, Brussels: Centre for European Reform.

Friis, K. (2000) 'From liminars to others: securitisation through myths', *Peace and Conflict Studies* 7(2): 1–17.

Fossum, J.E. and Schlesinger, P. (2007) *The European Union and the Public Sphere. A Communicative Space in the Making?* London: Routledge.

Garton Ash, T. (2007) 'Europe's true stories', *Prospect* 131, 25 February.

Gillespie, P. and Laffan, B. (2006) 'European identity: theory and empirics', in M. Cini and A.L. Bourne (eds), *Palgrave Advances in European Union Studies*, Basingstoke: Palgrave, pp. 131–50.

Graham, N. (1992) 'Habermas and the public sphere', in C. Calhoun (ed.), *The Media and the Public Sphere*, Cambridge, MA: MIT Press, pp. 109–42.

Grimm, D. (1995) 'Does Europe need a constitution?', *European Law Journal* 1(3): 282–302.

Grimm, D. (2005) 'Integration by constitution', *International Journal of Constitutional Law* 3(2–3): 193–208.

Habermas, J. (1995) 'Remarks on Dieter Grimm's "Does Europe need a constitution"', *European Law Journal* 1(3): 303–7.

Habermas, J. and Derrida, J. (2006) 'February 15, or what binds Europeans together: a plea for a common foreign policy, beginning at the core of Europe', in L. Thomassen (ed.), *The Derrida-Habermas Reader*, Edinburgh: University of Edinburgh Press, pp. 270–8.

Hague Summit (1969) Final communiqué of the Summit, available at http://aei.pitt.edu/1451/1/hague_1969.pdf (accessed 7 July 2011).

Hansen, L. (2005) *Security as Practice. Discourse Analysis and the Bosnian War*, London: Routledge.

Hinchman, L.P. and Hinchman, S.K. (1997) *Memory, Identity, Community. The Idea of Narrative in the Human Sciences*, Albany, NY: State University of NY Press.

Hopf, T. (2002) *Social Construction of International Politics. Identities and Foreign Policies, Moscow, 1955 & 1999*, New York: Cornell University Press.

Hyde Price, A. (2006) 'Normative power Europe: a realist critique', *Journal of European Public Policy* 13(2): 217–34.

Kagan, R. (2002) 'Power and weakness', *Washington Policy Review* 113 (June/July): 3–28.

Kevin, D. (2004) *Europe in the Media. A Comparison of Reporting, Representation and Rhetoric in National Media Systems in Europe*, London: Lawrence Erlbaum Associates.

Koh, H.H. (2003) 'America's Jekyl and Hyde exceptionalism', in M. Ignatieff (ed.), *American Exceptionalism and Human Rights*, Princeton, NJ: Princeton University Press, pp. 111–43.

Koopmans, R. and Pfetsch, B. (ed.) (2003) 'Towards a Europeanised public sphere? Comparing political actors and the media in Germany', *ARENA Working Paper* 03/23, available at http://www.sv.uio.no/arena/english/research/publications/arena-publications/workingpapers/working-papers2003/03_23.xml (accessed 14 September 2011).

Kux, S. and Sverdrup, U. (2000) 'Fuzzy borders and adaptive outsides: Norway, Switzerland and the EU', *Journal of European Integration* 22(4): 500–28.

Laclau, E. and Mouffe, C. (1985) *Hegemony and Socialist Strategy. Towards a Radical Democratic Politics*, London: Verso.

Lawler, P. (1997) 'Scandinavian exceptionalism and the European Union', *Journal of Common Market Studies* 35(4): 565–93.

Lazarus, N. (2004) 'The South African ideology: the myth of South African exceptionalism, the idea of renaissance', *The South Atlantic Quarterly* 103(4): 607–28.

Lee-Ohlsson, F. (2009) 'A bi-directional process of Europeanization', *Cooperation and Conflict* 22(2): 123–42.

Lipsett, S.M. (1996) *American Exceptionalism. A Double-Edged Sword*, New York: Norton.

Manners, I. (2002) 'Normative power Europe: a contradiction in terms?', *Journal of Common Market Studies* 40(2): 235–58.

Manners, I. (2006) 'The European Union as a normative power: a response to Thomas Diez', *Millennium* 35(1): 167–80.

Manners, I. (2010) 'Another Europe is possible: critical perspectives on European Union politics', in K.E. Jørgensen, M. Pollack and B. Rosamond (eds), *Handbook of European Union Politics*, London: Sage, pp. 77–96.

Manners, I. and Whitman, R. (2003) 'The "difference engine": constructing and representing the international identity of the European Union', *Journal of European Public Policy* 10(3): 380–404.

McSweeney, B. (1996) 'Identity and security: Buzan and the Copenhagen School', *Review of International Studies* 22(1): 82–93.

Meinhoff, U.H. (2004) 'Europe viewed from below: agents victims and the threat of the other', in R.K. Herman, T. Risse and M.B. Brewer (eds), *Transnational Identities: Becoming European in the EU*, Oxford: Rowman and Littlefield, pp. 214–44.

Müller-Brandeck-Bocquet, G. (2002) 'The new CFSP and ESDP decision-making system of the European Union', *European Foreign Affairs Review* 7(3): 275–82.

Neumann, I. (1999) *Uses of the Other. 'The East' in European Identity Formation*, Minneapolis, MN: University of Minneapolis Press.

Nicolaïdis, K. and Howse, R. (2002) '"This is my EUtopia ...": narrative as power', *Journal of Common Market Studies* 40(4): 767–92.

Palosaari, T. (2011) 'The art of adaptation: a study on the Europeanization of Finland's foreign and security policy', *TAPRI Studies in Peace and Conflict Research No. 96*, Tampere: Tampere University Press.

Pomorska, K. (2007) 'The impact of enlargement: Europeanisation of Polish foreign policy? Tracking adaptation and change in the Ministry of Foreign Affairs', *The Hague Journal of Diplomacy* 2(1): 25–51.

RECON (2008) 'Beyond intergovernmentalism and the quest for unity: democracy or efficiency?' RECON workshop programme for RECON workshop 'Beyond Intergovernmentalism and the Quest for Unity: Democracy or Efficiency?', Istanbul, 13–14 November 2008, available at http://www.reconproject.eu/projectweb/portalproject/IstanbulNov08_WorkshopOutline.html (accessed 14 September 2011).

Risse, T. (2001) 'A European identity: Europeanization and the evolution of nation state identities', in M.G. Cowles, J.A. Caporaso and T. Risse (eds), *Transforming Europe Europeanization and Domestic Change*, Ithaca, NY: Cornell University Press, pp. 198–216.

Risse, T. (2002) 'How do we know a European public sphere when we see one? Theoretical clarifications and empirical indicators', Paper presented at the IDNET Workshop 'Europeanisation and the Public Sphere', European University Institute, Florence, 21–22 February.

Risse, T. (2003) 'The Euro between national and European identity', *Journal of European Public Policy* 10(3): 487–505.

Risse, T. (2004) 'European institutions and identity change: what have we learned', in R.K Hermann, T. Risse Kappen and M.B Brewer (eds), *Transnational Identities. Becoming European in the EU*, Lanham, MD: Rowman and Littlefield, pp. 247–72.

Risse, T. and Grabowsky, J.K. (2008) 'European identity formation in the public sphere and in foreign policy', *RECON Online Working Paper 2008/04*, Oslo: ARENA, available at http://www.reconproject.eu/main.php/RECON_wp_0804.pdf?fileitem=16662546 (accessed 14 September 2011).

Scheipers, S. and Sicurelli, D. (2007) 'Normative power Europe: a credible Utopia?', *Journal of Common Market Studies* 45(2): 435–57.

Schlesinger, P. (1997) 'From cultural deference to political culture: media, politics and collective identity in the European Union', *Media, Culture & Society* 19(3): 369–91.

Schlesinger, P. (1999) 'Changing spaces of political communication: the case of the European Union', *Political Communication* 16(3): 263–79.

Semetko, H.A., de Vreese, C.H. and Peter, J. (2000) 'Europeanised politics – Europeanised media? European integration and political communication', *West European Politics* 23(4): 121–41.

Sifft, S. *et al.* (2007) 'Segmented Europeanization: exploring the legitimacy of the European Union from a public discourse perspective', *Journal of Common Market Studies* 45(1): 127–55.

Solana, J. (2003) *A Secure Europe in a Better World. The European Security Strategy*, Brussels, 12 December, available at http://www.consilium.europa.eu/uedocs/cmsUpload/78367.pdf (accessed 7 July 2011).

Stavridis, S. (2003) 'The Europeanisation of Greek foreign policy: a literature review', *Discussion Paper No.10*, London: The Hellenic Observatory, available at http://eprints.lse.ac.uk/5692/1/Stavridis-10.pdf (last 14 September 2011).

Tonra, B. (2001) *The Europeanisation of National Foreign Policy. Dutch, Danish and Irish Foreign Policy in the European Union*, London: Ashgate.

Tonra, B (2007) *Global Citizen and European Republic. Irish Foreign Policy in Transition*, Manchester: Manchester University Press.

Tonra, B. (2009) 'Democratic oversight over the Irish Government in the field of the Common Foreign and Security Policy', in G. Barrett (ed.), *National Parliaments and the European Union: The Constitutional Challenge for the Oireachtas and Other Member State Legislatures*, Dublin: Clarus Press, pp. 347–69.

Torreblanca, J.I. (2001) *The Reuniting of Europe. Promises, Negotiations and Compromises*, Aldershot: Ashgate.

Trenz, H.J. (2004) 'Media coverage on European governance: exploring the European public sphere in national quality newspapers', *European Journal of Communication* 19(3): 291–319.

Tully, J. (2007) 'A new kind of Europe? Democratic integration in the European Union', *Critical Review of International Social and Political Philosophy* 10(1): 71–86.

Ullock, C.J. (1996) 'Imagining community: a metaphysics of being or becoming', *Millenium Journal of International Studies* 25(2): 425–51.

van de Steeg, M (2002) 'Rethinking the conditions for a public sphere in the European Union', *European Journal of Social Theory* 5(4): 499–519.

Vale, P. and Taylor, I. (1999) 'South Africa's post-apartheid foreign policy five years on: from pariah state to "just another country"?', *The Round Table: The Commonwealth Journal of International Relations* 88(352): 629–34.

Waever, O. (1998) 'Insecurity, security and asecurity in the West European non-war community', in E. Adler and M. Barnett (eds), *Security Communities*, Cambridge: Cambridge University Press, pp. 69–118.

Waever, O. (2002) 'Identity, communities and foreign policy: discourse analysis as foreign policy theory', in L. Hansen and O. Waever (eds), *European Integration and National Identity: The Challenge of the Nordic States*, London: Routledge, pp. 20–49.

Whitman, R. (2010) *The European Neighbourhood Policy in Perspective*, Palgrave Studies in European Union Politics, London: Palgrave.

Wong, R. (2005) 'The Europeanization of foreign policy', in C. Hill and M. Smith (eds), *International Relations and the European Union*, Oxford: Oxford University Press, pp. 134–53.

Wong, R. (2006) *The Europeanization of French Foreign Policy. France and the EU in East Asia*, New York: Palgrave Macmillan.

Zimmerman, H. (2007) 'Realist power Europe? The EU in the negotiations about China's and Russia's WTO accession', *Journal of Common Market Studies* 45(4): 813–32.

Index

Page numbers in *Italics* represent tables.
Page numbers in **Bold** represent figures.
Page numbers followed by n represent endnotes.

For Product Safety Concerns and Information please contact our EU
representative GPSR@taylorandfrancis.com
Taylor & Francis Verlag GmbH, Kaufingerstraße 24, 80331 München, Germany

9 781138 107366